Robyn Wrigley-Carr is Ass
Spirituality at Alphacrucis Coll
Professor of the Public and Contextual Research Centre at Charles
Sturt University, Australia. Her doctorate, at the University of
St Andrews, examined Baron Friedrich von Hügel as a spiritual
director. As well as being an academic, Robyn is a spiritual director
and retreat leader. She is author of *The Spiritual Formation of Evelyn
Underhill* and the editor of *Evelyn Underhill's Prayer Book*. Robyn is
on the editorial board and Book Reviews Editor for the *Journal for
the Study of Spirituality* and on the Executive for the International
Network for the Study of Spirituality.

In memory of Dr Caroline Julia Batchelder,
much-loved friend and colleague
(9 April 1961–30 March 2021)

Music of Eternity

of

Eternity

MEDITATIONS
FOR ADVENT WITH
EVELYN UNDERHILL

ROBYN WRIGLEY-CARR

First published in Great Britain in 2021

Society for Promoting Christian Knowledge
36 Causton Street
London SW1P 4ST
www.spck.org.uk

British Library Cataloguing-in-Publication Data
A catalogue record for this book is available from the British Library

ISBN 978-0-281-08550-7
eBook ISBN 978-0-281-08551-4

Typeset by Falcon Oast Graphic Art Ltd

eBook by Falcon Oast Graphic Art Ltd

Contents

Contents

Part 4

HOLY LIVING: EMBRACING GOD'S COMING (GOD HAS COME!)

Foreword

I am delighted to offer this wonderful book by Robyn as my Advent book for 2021. It comes with heartfelt gratitude to Robyn, and to Evelyn. But it also comes with a warning – do not start to read unless you are ready to be compelled to continue!

Almost before I had begun, I was hooked. In the very first reflection, these words of Evelyn are quoted: 'You know that there are better melodies.' There can be few better summings-up of the hunger our hearts have for beauty, for adventure, for resolution, for consolation, joy, unity, and for the heart-breaking and heart-mending power of heaven's music.

This book has sharpened my hunger for God's presence, and helped me to depend more on him for the satisfaction of that hunger; it has encouraged me to listen harder, and reminded me that God's symphony is all around me. It has invited me to be still, and to wait in the stillness; it has helped me to re-examine the hardships of this past year, and to find Christ at work in unseen corners. It has set before me a feast of resources and gentle encouragement to enter into adoration and, tellingly, it has increased in me the desire for others to hear this eternal music for themselves.

I hope these reflections will help you to find in the welcoming, awaiting, recognising and embracing of God's advent the stirrings of the perfect music of His love and His kingdom, present and arriving.

This Advent season, as we enter consciously into the waiting between God's promise and its fulfilment once more, I pray that every joy we find in earthly music may be multiplied many times over in our spirits, as we make space and prepare our inward ears to hear the stirring of the heavenly melody. As we join the song of the angels this Christmas, may our lives, as well as our voices, be tuned to that melody, so that we not only hear it, but also carry it into the restless world to which God is still – and always – coming.

Amen. Come, Lord Jesus!

Stephen Cottrell
Archbishop of York

Prologue

Receiving means to keep ourselves carefully tuned in, sensitive to the music of Eternity.

We can never adore enough.[1]

(Evelyn Underhill)

The moment I was asked to write this book, my head and heart were flooded with the melody, 'O come let us adore Him!' – an apt line from a Christmas carol, given Evelyn Underhill's repeated emphasis on adoration as our essential response to God. Evelyn reminds us that to receive God, we need to be attentively listening for the music of Eternity. She had a plaque embroidered with the word 'ETERNITY' in her study, as a constant, visual reminder of God – the unseen reality, the Eternal song. But how do we tune in to this barely audible, subtle music – these Eternal symphonies?

Advent and the run-up to Christmas can be a noisy, busy frenzy of shopping and social events that drown out any gentle preparation for the coming of the Christ-child. This may also be a time when our thoughts turn to loved ones we have lost, whether through death or fractured relationships, and we are conscious of empty chairs at the Christmas table. Evelyn tells one friend who's struggling, 'I do hope your Invisible Christmas will be full of the Lord even though the Visible part may be rather difficult.'[2] Whatever pain the Christmas season might amplify for us, Evelyn invites us to have 'a little touch of Eternity in amongst the rush'.[3]

Advent is one of the great holy seasons of the Christian calendar, when we're drawn into the experience of a young, pregnant, Jewish woman awaiting the coming of her baby: *Emmanuel*. God has remembered His promise to generations of Old Testament believers, and the coming of Christ is the end of their long, long wait for a Messiah. Mary is told, 'You will give birth to a Son – call Him Jesus.' And, unlike other biblical figures given similar promises (Abram, Sarai and Zechariah), the young Mary does not laugh or doubt or struggle. There seems to be only amazement and surprise: 'How will this be?' The angel explains and, astonishingly, Mary's response is one of simple, profound faith and obedience: 'Let it be to me according to Your word.' She's 'bursting with God-news' and 'dancing the song' of her Saviour God (Luke 1.46–47, MSG). God has come with a promise and Mary accepts the word and becomes the bearer of God. But the child is not only formed, known and ushered into the world by God, but somehow, paradoxically, *is* God. God *Himself* is born!

Advent is a season of great human experience, one of expectant faith between what God has begun and what He is yet to complete. We wait between two Divine actions: a promise and its fulfilment. God's prevenience (from *pre-*, 'before', and *ven-*, 'to come') – the idea that He is the initiator, the prime mover, who is always present at the scene before we arrive – underlaid Evelyn's theology and led her to expect God to act. He initiates before we as humans ever engage in action. And even where we do get involved, we are simply *participating* in His work. We act in small submissive ways, supporting the action of God, willingly drawn into the drama of God, involved in what He is doing. We wait and watch, listen and speak, pray and worship. Our posture needs to be one of receiving and surrendering to the priority of God.[4] Evelyn urges us to embody this spirit of Advent every day, not only during the season, for God's comings (plural) are perpetual: 'Many a song have I sung . . . all their notes have always proclaimed, "He comes, comes, ever comes."'[5] We may sometimes feel too distracted and sleepy to notice, but we can wake up and be attentive!

Evelyn Underhill (1875–1941) has much to offer us this Advent season if we desire to listen, observe and attend to God. Evelyn was a married Englishwoman who lived most of her life in London. She wrote nearly 40 books and hundreds of articles, and received an honorary doctorate from the University of Aberdeen. But it wasn't her deep intellect and creative flair that primarily drew people to her: she radiated love. Spiritually intuitive, perceptive and discerning, Evelyn was fun to be around, with a cheeky sense of humour. Though she grew up in a secular household, Evelyn had a deep appreciation of beauty, both in the wonder of creation and in religious art, and a fascination with 'unseen reality'. She wrote several works on mysticism and the Christian mystics but it was only when she reached midlife that she encountered Christ. Evelyn describes it as like 'watching the sun rise very slowly – and then suddenly one knew what it was'.[6] The New Testament, which she had never really been able to work out, suddenly seemed full of things previously unnoticed, and partaking of the Eucharist took on a new, rich significance. From this point, Evelyn wrote books about the spiritual life and led spiritual retreats, becoming a highly distinguished spiritual director. She wore her Anglicanism 'with a difference'.[7] Describing herself as a 'scamp . . . unable to crystallise into the official shape' and the cat of 'any other Colour in a cat show', Evelyn was very ecumenical. She believed the most profound enemy of Christianity was anything that made it 'narrow'.[8] Despite this openness, Evelyn kept herself anchored and grounded through her strong focus upon Christ.

As Evelyn leads us on our Advent journey – a season of Divine action and initiative, interwoven with human response – it might be helpful to visualise a dance in four stages:

1 Prevenience: welcoming God's coming – God is at work and draws us into His coming action (God *is*!) [God]
2 Advent: awaiting God's coming – our expectant participation (Christ is coming!) [Our response]
3 *Emmanuel*: recognising God's coming – God acts to fulfil His promises (God comes!) [Christ]

3

4 Holy living: embracing God's coming (God has come!) [Our response]

In Part 1, our focus is on God and His love. Evelyn encourages us to see all of life in relation to God, rather than God in relation to life.[9] 'He is' and everything flows from that reality (making a spirituality that starts with and focuses on the self not only dangerous but pointless).[10] So we begin with God – His perpetual coming to us, His reality in and of Himself – and we consider the wonderful concept of the mighty symphony of the Triune God. Then we ponder God as the Eternal Love brooding over creation and our lives, trying to be alert to His action – listening, watching, waiting, so we know how to participate. We close Part 1 reflecting upon two phrases of the Lord's Prayer that dwell on praising God in worship: 'Father, hallowed be Your Name' and 'Your Kingdom come'.

Part 2 focuses on Advent as we await God's coming in the person of Christ. For us, as for Mary, Advent is a season lived between two worlds – the seen, external, busy world, and the unseen, internal, spiritual world, where the Spirit works in tranquillity, creating the life of Eternity in us. Our role is largely one of being attentive and watching for the signs of God's work, as we continue to live our lives within this context. In these excerpts Evelyn provides reflective insights concerning waiting, expectancy, hope, silence, prayer, meditation and contemplation. As we anticipate the arrival of the Christ-child, we engage in these quieter, more reflective types of prayer.

Part 3 focuses on *Emmanuel* – God with us – recognising God's coming in Christ. I have deliberately made this section the longest because Christ is the one we're waiting for and we need time and space to gaze upon and listen to Him. As we humbly look at Christ, and dwell in prayer on His person and words, His life unfolds, disclosing more of the truth it holds.[11] We journey with Christ through His birth, temptations, rescuing miracles, transfiguration, service, suffering and Emmaus walk, before closing with His glorification.

Part 4 is about holy living – our response to all that God has done as we embrace His coming in Christ, and His continual coming to us in every moment. In this section we cover some of the essential responses to our Triune God outlined by Evelyn – adoration, partaking of the Eucharist, sacrifice, humility, love, forgiveness and peace.

Our Epilogue takes us back to Eternity, where we began with the Triune God's mighty symphony. As we stand here, between the already and the not yet, our 'ears' need to be 'awake' to 'listen to the Wind Words, the Spirit blowing through the churches'. We who are 'thirsty' say 'Come' (Revelation 2.7, 11, 17, 29; 22.17, MSG). And as we strain to hear that music of Eternity and give ourselves as participants in God's Eternal song, we may echo the beautiful words of John Donne: 'I shall be made Your music – as I come.'[12]

Note: In this text Evelyn's excerpts have been adapted. An * denotes a new reference in the excerpt. Details regarding editing and references are outlined at the back of this book. I wish to acknowledge an ADM Senior Research Fellowship that enabled me to write this book.

Part 1

PREVENIENCE: WELCOMING GOD'S COMING (GOD *IS*)

In Part 1, our focus is God – His perpetual coming to us, His mighty symphony as the Triune God, and His initiating action in the creation around us and in our lives. We close with Evelyn's reflections upon two lines from the Lord's Prayer, where Jesus models to us adoration of God.

1

God's perpetual coming

In Advent 1940, just months before her death, Underhill reminded her prayer group that God constantly comes to His people. However, if our lives are filled with activities and noise, it won't be easy to hear the barely audible music of God's loving Presence! He often comes softly, in places and ways that surprise us, and His comings are rarely what we expect, so we generally miss their 'earthly disguise'. Cultivating a spirit of Advent is essential, for our spiritual lives depend on God's perpetual coming to us. Evelyn encourages us to learn the art of listening to the Spirit's whisper.[1] This involves attentive waiting and watching for what God is doing among us and within us, and humble, eager expectancy, so we can welcome, notice and celebrate God's coming.

> The world is full of jangling noises. You know that there are better melodies. But you will never transmit the heavenly music to others unless you yourselves are tuned in to it . . . giving . . . it careful and undivided attention during part of each day . . . you must yourselves be spiritually alive.[2]

> God is love . . . We love because He first loved us.
> (1 John 4.16, 19, NIV)

> Keep company with GOD . . . Quiet down before GOD, be prayerful before Him . . . Wait passionately for GOD, don't leave the path . . . There's a future in strenuous wholeness . . . The spacious, free life is from GOD, it's also protected and safe . . . when we run to Him, He saves us.
> (Psalm 37.4, 7, 34, 38–40, MSG)

*What is the great lesson of Advent? It's the many-sided truth of God's perpetual coming to His creatures in secret and humble ways; the nearness of His saving care and energising grace. 'Have you not heard His silent steps? He comes, comes, ever comes.'[3] At the beginning of her course the Church looks out towards Eternity, and realises her own poverty and imperfection and her utter dependence on this perpetual coming of God.

Advent is, of course, first of all a preparation for Christmas; which commemorates God's saving entrance into history in the Incarnation of Jesus Christ. 'For while all things were in quiet silence, and the night was in the midst of her swift course, Your Almighty Word leaped down from heaven out of Your royal throne.'[4] Alleluia.

A tremendous spiritual event then took place; something that disclosed the very nature of God and His relation to His universe. But there was little to show for it on the surface of life. All people saw was a poor girl unconditionally submitted to God's Will, and a baby born in difficult circumstances. And this contrast between the outward appearance and the inner reality is true of all the comings of God to us. We must be very loving and very alert if we want to recognise them in their earthly disguise. Again and again He comes and the revelation is not a bit what we expect.

So the next lesson Advent should teach us is that our attitude towards Him should always be one of humble, eager expectancy. Our spiritual life depends on His perpetual coming to us, far more than on our going to Him. Every time a channel is made for Him He comes; every time our hearts are open to Him He enters, bringing a fresh gift of His very life, and on that life we depend. We should think of the whole power and splendour of God as always pressing in upon our small souls. 'In Him we live, and move, and have our being' (Acts 17.28, KJV). But that power and splendour mostly reach us in homely, inconspicuous ways; in the sacraments, and in our prayers, joys and sorrows and in all opportunities of loving service. This means that one of the most important things in our prayer is the eager confidence with which we throw ourselves open to His perpetual coming. There should always be more waiting than striving in a Christian's prayer – an absolute dependence on the self-giving charity of God.

The old Advent collects of the Church are full of this sense of our need and of God perpetually coming with His gifts to purify, enrich and redeem: 'We ask You, O Lord, to cleanse our minds by Your daily visitation. Let our souls be kindled by Your Spirit; that being filled as lamps by the Divine Gift, we may shine like blazing lights before the Presence of Your Son Christ at His coming.'

As we draw near Christmas, this sense of our own need and of the whole world's need of God's coming – never greater perhaps than it is now – becomes more intense. In the great Advent Antiphons, which are said in the week before Christmas, we seem to hear the voice of the whole suffering creation saying, 'Come! Give us wisdom, give us light, deliver us, liberate us, lead us, teach us how to live. Save us.' And we, joining in that prayer, unite our need with the one need of the whole world. We have to remember that the answer to the prayer was not a new, wonderful world order, but Bethlehem and the Cross: a life of complete surrender to God's Will; and we must expect this answer to be worked out in our own lives in terms of humility and sacrifice.

If our lives are ruled by this spirit of Advent, this loving expectation of God, we will have a quality quite different from that of conventional piety. For we will be centred on an entire and conscious dependence upon the supernatural love that supports us; hence all self-confidence will be destroyed in us and replaced by perfect confidence in God. We will be docile to His pressure, and obedient to every indication of His Will.

'I am not a God afar off, I am Your Maker and Friend' (Jeremiah 23.23). This is one of the great lessons of Christmas and its realisation in our own lives is a principal object of Christian prayer.

*Attention to God is the primary religious act. Our thoughts of Him are often pitiably thin, narrow, conventional. Ourselves, our works, our anxieties slip into the centre of the picture and God becomes merely the source of energy for carrying on our activities. There are a great deal too many who merely utilise prayer. We are so obsessed by the importance of our work, our friends and our interests. If we put His worship last and our needs first, all proportion goes. Then, instead of the expansion that comes from selfless adoration, our souls contract.

He is calling you, demanding your complete surrender in order that you may become completed persons. Nothing matters but that demand and your soul's response. The essence of life is that response, whether made in work or in prayer. Augustine's great saying is so appropriate here: 'God is the only Reality and we are only real insofar as we are in Him and He in us.'

Only a spiritual disposition which thus puts the whole emphasis on God, perpetually turning to God and losing itself in God, is safe. Only this disposition escapes a Christianity that dwells on its work and tries to use God's Power for its chosen activity. Once we have given ourselves to God, His action transcends, precedes and controls our own, and goes on all the time, whether we are aware of it or not. The central point governing the work that any soul can do for God *and* other souls is its attitude to Him, its relationship to Him, its self-oblivious adoration.

For discussion

- How do you find yourself responding to the idea that God constantly comes to us in unexpected, disguised and inconspicuous ways?
- Can you think of an instance recently when God might have been trying to awaken you to His Presence – to His 'comings'?
- What resonated with you in these two excerpts? Why?

Prayer

Thank You, God, that You keep coming to me, though I often miss the secret and humble ways in which You do so. Please forgive me for being distracted by busyness or things that are not really important, and for the times I've ignored You. Make me lovingly expectant of Your coming to me this Advent. Open my eyes, unblock my ears and enable me to slow down so I can recognise, welcome and respond to Your comings. Help me to imagine you as the Choirmaster of my life, and come and dwell within me, in Jesus' name, Amen.

2
Mighty symphony of the Triune God

Evelyn sees this Advent theme of God's perpetual coming in quiet, hidden ways, as playing out through *all* of creation. We begin with Eternity, the God of Love, and this Triune God – Father, Son and Spirit – self-expresses as a mighty, symphonic dance, filling the Universe! As Evelyn wrote, 'Before our stellar universe, this Triune fire of Love was already lighted; creation itself being an act of love'.[1] But we are largely deaf to God's elusive music and the melodies to be found in the ordinary, everyday moments of our lives. In becoming more attentive, we may well begin to hear a phrase now and again ... Opening ourselves to God will save us from living narrow, constricted lives, and as we lose ourselves and find the courage to say 'Come!', we will grow to become 'pure capacity' for God.[2] Welcoming God will involve shifting focus from 'Mine' to 'Ours', for we're all linked as we respond in worship to our Triune God.

> Enrichment of the sense of God is surely the crying need of our current Christianity. A shallow . . . brightly varnished this-world faith . . . [is a] ruling defect of institutional religion . . . We are drifting towards a religion which consciously or unconsciously keeps its eye on humanity rather than on Deity – which lays all the stress on service, and hardly any of the stress on awe: and that is a type of religion, which in practice does not wear well . . . in those awful moments when the pain and mystery of life are most deeply felt . . . It does not lead to sanctity.[3]

Once again I'll go over what GOD has done, lay out on the
table the ancient wonders; I'll ponder all the things You've
accomplished, and give a long, loving look at Your acts.
O God! Your way is holy! No god is great like God! You're the
God who makes things happen.
(Psalm 77.11–14, MSG)

God is love. Whoever lives in love lives in God, and God in
them.
(1 John 4.16, NIV)

*So many Christians are like deaf people at a concert. They study
the programme carefully, believe every statement made in it, speak
respectfully of the music, but only really hear a phrase now and
again. So they have no notion of the mighty symphony that fills
the universe, to which our lives are destined to make their tiny
contribution, the self-expression of the Eternal God. Yet there are
plenty of things in our normal experience that imply the existence
of that music, that life.

Any mature person, looking back on their own life, will be forced
to recognise factors that can't be attributed to personal initiative
or mere chance. It's as if a hidden, directive power – personal, living,
free – were working through circumstances and often against our
intention or desire; pressing us in a certain direction, and moulding
us beneath the surface of life, which generally contents us. There
are unsuspected deeps and great spiritual forces which condition
and control our small lives. Some people become sensitive to the
pressure of these forces. The rest of us easily ignore the evidence for
this whole realm of experience, because it's so hidden and interior;
and we're so busy responding to obvious, outward things. When we
take it seriously, it surely suggests that we're essentially spiritual as
well as natural creatures; and that therefore life in its fullness must
involve correspondence not only with our visible, ever-changing

environment, but also with our invisible, unchanging one: the Spirit of all spirits, God, in whom we live and move and have our being. The significance, the greatness of humanity, consists in our ability to do this. When we lift our eyes from the crowded bypass to the eternal hills, then, how much the personal and practical things we have to deal with are enriched. What meaning and coherence comes into our scattered lives.

We mostly spend those lives conjugating three verbs: to Want, to Have and to Do. Craving, clutching and fussing, on the material, political, social, emotional, intellectual – even on the religious – plane, we are kept in perpetual unrest: forgetting that none of these verbs has any ultimate significance, except so far as it's transcended by, and included in, the fundamental verb, to Be: and that Being, not wanting, having and doing, is the essence of a spiritual life. But now, with this widening of the horizon, our personal ups and downs, desires, cravings, efforts, are seen in scale; as small, transitory spiritual facts, within a vast, abiding spiritual world and lit by a steady, spiritual light. And at once a new coherence comes into our existence, a new tranquillity and release. Like a chalet in the Alps, that homely existence gains atmosphere, dignity and significance from the greatness of the sky above it and the background of the everlasting hills.

The people of our time are helpless, distracted and rebellious, unable to interpret what is happening, and full of apprehension about what is to come, largely because they've lost this sure hold on the Eternal; which gives to each life meaning, direction and steadiness, that sense of ultimate security which only a hold on the Eternal brings. It delivers us from all niggling fuss about ourselves, and prevents us from feeling self-important about our own little spiritual adventures.

Dante says that directly a soul ceases to say 'Mine', and says 'Ours', it makes the transition from the narrow, constricted, individual life to the truly free, personal, creative, spiritual life; in which all are linked together in one single response to the Father of all spirits, God. Here, all interpenetrate and all, however humble and obscure their lives may seem, can and do affect each other. Every advance made by one is made for all. Only when we recognise all this, and act on it, are we fully alive, taking our proper place in the universe of spirits.

Spiritual life, which is profoundly organic, means the give and take, the willed correspondence of the little human spirit with the Infinite Spirit, here where it is; its feeding upon Him, its growth towards perfect union with Him, its response to His attraction and subtle pressure. That growth and that response may seem to us like a movement, a journey which is more like the inevitable movement of the iron filing to the great magnet attracting it. The overruling reality of life is the Will and Choice of a Spirit acting not in a mechanical but in a living, personal way.

*The French contemplative Lucie-Christine says that when the voice of God called her, it was at one and the same time a Light, a Drawing and a Power. What we have in the doctrine of the Trinity is above all the crystallisation and mind's interpretation of these three ways in which our simple contact with God is actualised by us. What is that supernal symphony of which this elusive music, with its three complementary strains, forms part? We cannot know. But even those strains that we do hear, assure us how far we are yet from conceiving the possibilities of life, power and beauty, contained in them.

*As our life comes to maturity, we discover to our confusion that human ears can pick up from the Infinite many incompatible tunes, but can't hear the whole symphony. And the melody confided to our care, the one which we alone perhaps can contribute and which taxes our powers to the full, has in it not only the notes of triumph but also the notes of pain. An unconditional surrender to the Divine Will, a little silence and leisure. A great deal of faithfulness, kindness and courage. All this is within the reach of anyone who cares enough for it to pay the price.

*Prayer associates us with that creative and supporting Love, keeps us plastic to the pressure of the moulding Charity. The very best we are likely to achieve in the world of prayer will be a small part in a mighty symphony; not a peculiarly interesting duet. When our devotional life seems to us to have become a duet, we should listen more carefully. Then we shall hear a greater music, within which that little melody of ours can find its place.

For discussion

- Can you detect 'melodies of God' playing in your life or that of others? If so, what helps you recognise these?
- In what parts of your life might you need to shift from 'Mine' to 'Ours'?
- Spend the day attentively listening to your life and to the encounters you have with people and creation. Notice where and how you sense strains of God's mighty symphony.

Prayer

Lord, I often feel the lack of Your Presence and action in my life. Please draw me to You, Father, Son and Spirit, and the glorious complementary strains of Your elusive music. Reveal to me what is making me slow to hear and obey Your call, and enable me to loosen my hold on unhelpful distractions and enticements in my life so I can shift from 'Mine' to 'Ours' and generously give to those around me. Teach me to know You and to sing in praise of Your Eternal might and loveliness, in Jesus' name, Amen.

3

Eternal Love brooding over creation

We move from the Triune God, complete in Himself, to gazing upon His work in creation. The Creator God – the loving Eternal Artist – contemplates myriad, unformed possibilities, with patient, fostering love. And this same creative Spirit continues to brood over our broken world, as we struggle with the recent pandemic, with poverty and war, with racism, with the potential effects of climate change and many other challenges. Yet slowly, gently, lovingly, God draws our souls to become a reflection of His holy beauty. And not only our souls, but also those of all who are connected with us, for within them, too, the Holy Spirit is brooding. Evelyn sees creation as the continuing action of a personal, self-spending Love, and the outward events of our lives can be understood only in relation to that unseen Love, as it penetrates and supports us. The God we thirst for, yet also resist, faithfully works to transform our self-centred desires as creatures, into the 'wide-spreading, outpouring love' of citizens of Heaven.[1] This is a Triune God of ongoing re-creation.

> De Caussade: The Divine action bathes the whole universe. It penetrates all creatures, it hovers above them. Wherever they are, it is. It goes before them, it is with them, it follows them. They need but let themselves be borne upon its waves.[2]

> Is there any place I can go to avoid Your Spirit? To be out of Your sight? . . . You formed me in my mother's womb. I thank You, High God – You're breathtaking! Body and soul, I am

marvellously made! I worship in adoration – what a creation! You know me inside and out . . . exactly how I was made, bit by bit, how I was sculpted from nothing into something.
(Psalm 139.7, 13–15, MSG)

First this: God created the Heavens and Earth – all you see, all you don't see. Earth was a soup of nothingness, a bottomless emptiness, an inky blackness. God's Spirit brooded like a bird above the watery abyss. God spoke: 'Light!' And light appeared.
(Genesis 1.1–3, MSG)

*Consider this picture from the great biblical poem of creation. Darkness, chaos, mystery: yet, already manifest, the first of all energies, the cherishing, loving action of God. Love brooding on the formless, unpromising deeps – patient, fostering action on the restless, unformed, chaotic, empty world. Bit by bit, the tranquil, brooding Spirit draws forth beauty, wonder, variety of life, as a great musician on a theme. That long, brooding quiet, when nothing seems to happen – *this* is a great part of the action of creation. The Eternal Artist, Eternal Love, is at work. The patient, loving, Presence of God, by His ceaseless action, gives form – bringing forth life.

The Holy Spirit *now* broods over the bent world: giving life, bringing beauty, significance, holiness; creating from chaos the Kingdom of God – all possibilities unrealised, till the first mover of all things, moved.

Take this into our own souls – that confused, formless, inner life. Lord, perhaps we *can* dare to look into these dark waters beyond the surface where we usually live, to the mysterious reality of our being which lies open to Your action and brooding pressure of Love. The possibilities of our souls, as You see them, are infinite, because they're only limited by Your creative power. You desire to realise *all* those possibilities – make us a pure reflection of Your holy beauty. Each of our chaotic, troubled souls is *meant* to be a Promise of Your

Glory, flowering before You, unfolding the treasures You've planted in the darkness – display them in Your Light.

We don't live as though this *were* the meaning and intention of our life. We give all our attention to the troubled surface of the waters, taking that very seriously – ruffled by winds of hope, fear, love and hate. Yet those have little to do with the life of prayer – they merely distract from its real business. All those fluctuations of feeling all count very little against the steady, brooding action of Your Will.

In the world of prayer, these surface movements, these self-occupied efforts, effect nothing. They leave our soul's true-being empty and formless. Only You can fill it, giving it form. Sometimes something warns us that our real part is to keep quiet: that You don't want intelligent, energetic Christians doing jobs in their own way, then offering them to You: what You want is *stripped, formless souls*, utterly subservient to the hidden operation of Your Love: souls on which You can exercise Your deepest creative action, and add to the Cross.

Perhaps in those depths of our being there are secrets hidden, desires and tendencies we dare not acknowledge, even to ourselves. Enter – burn, purify. We can't help ourselves. We wait upon You. Our restless minds achieve nothing; Your unwavering pressure does all.

Come! Brood on our turbulent, rebellious, indecisive wills – make them the channels of Your Will. On our distracted, troubled minds, restless emotions – subordinate them to Your overruling love. Come! Spirit of Love! Penetrate and transform us by the action of Your purifying life. May Your constant, brooding love bring forth in us more love. Give us grace to remain still under Your action; may humble stillness be our prayer.

My small, formless, imperfect soul is constantly subject to the loving, creative action of God, in all the bustle of my daily life, its anxieties, tensions and dreary, unspiritual stretches – gradually giving its ordained form and significance. All the events of my life are ways in which I experience His pressure.

21

I review my life in the stillness, from this viewpoint, deepening my gratitude and awe. In every joy, grief, sacrifice, temptation, opportunity or relationship – I feel Your delicate touch and personal action. So my true life consists, not in self-development or self-chosen achievement, but in an ever-increasing correspondence with Your Life – loving, humble, recognition and acceptance of the Spirit's action – especially when it prevents my best intentions, changing the shape of the creature I thought I'd be. What has all this to do with my prayer? *Everything*.

In prayer, my soul and God draw near – His fullness to my emptiness. If I realise a little of His Spirit working in my deeps, His action is most directly felt. All my prayer must be penetrated by this sense of my helpless imperfection, quiet abandonment of my formless soul to the Spirit brooding on the waters, bringing order, if I yield to His action. Without God's grace I'm chaos. With that grace I'm a tiny bit of the Spiritual World being organised for His service. Come! Creator Spirit! Fill with grace the hearts You've created.

So, what matters most in my prayer is not my desires, feelings, asking, efforts – not even my poor little bit of worship: but *God*, Who calls forth these stirrings of life. God, the Master of the Tides, changing and creating me, bringing, out of my unpromising depths, surprises of His wisdom and love; because my tiny will has made a slight response to His Mighty Will. 'You have fashioned me behind and before and laid Your hands on me' (Psalm 139.5).

Now we turn to souls with whom we're linked, for whom we must pray. We see them, too, without form, void; they often seem empty of love, trust and adoration; turbulent, uneasy, lacking meaning and loveliness – given over to ceaseless activity; at the mercy of every wind and current; and in their restlessness, so unpromising, so recalcitrant to God. Such easy subjects for our pessimistic indifference, but they too are part of Your raw material. Infinite possibilities are hidden in their deeps. There, too, Your Holy Spirit is brooding with cherishing power, bringing forth unrealised possibilities of life.

Keep in my mind Your invisible action and Presence, where it's most difficult to see – in the callous, greedy, earthly minded, flippant, cocksure; check my arrogance, intolerance, lack of patient, confident love. Keep in my mind the boundless possibilities of life, power and beauty hidden in every soul: and Your untiring, loving patience. I'm ignorant of these restless lives surrounding me. You've taken the turbulent, unharmonious, sinful, rebellious; and have created Your saints. Teach me to await Your creative action on other souls, and especially in those I'm tempted to dislike or neglect. Teach me reverence for all that unformed human nature on which Your Holy Spirit rests, which You can penetrate, transform, make holy, and in which You did deign to be incarnate, and showed us the Father's glory.

For discussion

- Where do you see hints of God's ongoing re-creation in your life, in your community and in the world?
- How might you join in with what God is doing in these places?
- What are those 'secrets hidden, desires and tendencies' that you dare not acknowledge, even to yourself? Ask God to reveal them to you.

Prayer

Come, Creator Spirit! Come cleanse my heart, lay Your sacred hands on me and transform me. I want to discover Your purposes for my life, to have perfect confidence in You, and to be content to dwell in the warm darkness of Your fostering love. I praise You, God, for You are beyond me, yet also in me, beneath me and above me. I thank You for patiently, gently, creating me and constantly sustaining me. Lord, teach me my new song and my new name, in Jesus' name, Amen.

4

Wakening to God's Eternal Action

From gazing at God's action in creation, we now look more fully at how God works through history and in our lives. The biblical narrative vividly conveys that each event we experience is directly linked to God's quiet action.[1] God acts first and we respond, just as we love because He first loved us. Sometimes we may feel God working in us quietly and feel renewed or steadied as a result. On other occasions, God's dramatic action may have a compelling, convicting effect.[2] Usually God reveals Himself gently, for we could not bear His awe-filled beauty.[3] The assurance that God is always the initiator, that all that really matters is done 'to' us, not 'by' us, made Evelyn alert to the ways in which God continually presses in on our souls, pouring out His love.[4] Our world is completely penetrated by God, and we're invited to respond, like Mary, to His ongoing action.

> The . . . spontaneity, the exercise of our limited freedom – genuinely ours . . . are yet entirely dependent on this prevenient and overruling Presence, acting with power and gentleness in the soul's ground. Progress in prayer is perhaps most safely measured by our increasing recognition of this action, the extent in which the Spirit 'prays in us' and we co-operate with it . . . the action of God is always felt to deepen, stimulate and direct the self's own action – never to abolish it.[5]

I sing to GOD, the Praise-Lofty, and find myself safe and saved . . . He stood me up on a wide-open field; I stood there

saved – surprised to be loved! GOD made my life complete when I placed all the pieces before Him . . . Now I'm alert to GOD's ways . . . Every day I review the ways He works . . . GOD rewrote the text of my life when I opened the book of my heart to His eyes.
(Psalm 18.3, 19–20, 22, 24, MSG)

We love because He first loved us.
(1 John 4.19, NIV)

*There's constantly implied in the religious outlook of the Old and New Testament writers, the expected invasion of another order over against the historical and human. Here, Spirit always represents the intervention of the very Life of God. The biblical world is not wholly built up by the quiet action of aqueous deposits. It witnesses to volcanic periods; when another order intervenes, with power to compel and transform. 'The Holy Spirit will come on you, and the power of the Most High will overshadow you' (Luke 1.35, NIV) – one order acting on and through another order; the whole human scene subject to the free, mysterious action of a Creative Power. The life of prayer hinges on it. The Church's great hymn to the Spirit, 'The Golden Sequence', beginning with the word *Come*, presents the essence of biblical religion.

*Most of our conflicts and difficulties come from trying to deal with the spiritual and practical aspects of our life separately, instead of realising them as parts of one whole. If our practical life is centred on our own interests, cluttered by possessions, distracted by ambitions, passions, wants and worries, beset by a sense of our own rights, importance, anxieties or longings for success, we need not expect our spiritual life will be a contrast. Only when the conviction – not merely the idea – that the demand of the Spirit, however inconvenient, comes first and IS first, rules the whole of it, will those objectionable noises die down, which drown the quieter voices by their din. God is All. He alone matters.

Our spiritual life is His affair. It consists in being drawn, at His pace, in His way, to the place where He wants us to be; not the place we fancied for ourselves. For the most part, the presence and action of the great spiritual universe surrounding us is no more noticed by us than the pressure of air on our bodies, or the action of light. Our field of attention isn't wide enough, our spiritual senses not sufficiently alert. Most people work so hard developing their correspondence with the visible world, their power of corresponding with the invisible is rudimentary. But when we begin to wake a little and notice that spiritual light and spiritual atmosphere, the whole situation changes – our horizon widened, our experience enormously enriched, our responsibilities enlarged. Our values begin to change, then we do. Here God's creative action on a human creature enters a new phase. Each human spirit is an unfinished product, on which the Creative Spirit is always at work.

The moment we become aware of God's creative action, able to respond or resist, is when our conscious spiritual life begins. Bit by bit the inexorable pressure is applied, and bit by bit the soul responds; until it realises the landscape has been transformed – seen in a new proportion, lit by a new light. There's always the sense we're concerned with two realities, not one. What matters most and takes precedence is the fact of a living Reality over against humanity, Who stoops towards humanity, and first incites, then supports and responds to its seeking. It's through this strange communion between the creature human and the Creator God that the spiritual life develops in depth and power.

The development of the spiritual life involves attending to God, then getting our tangled, half-real psychic lives – so tightly coiled about ourselves and our interests, including our spiritual interests – into harmony with God's great movement. Mortification means killing the roots of self-love – pride, possessiveness, anger, violence, ambition, greed in all their disguises, however respectable those disguises – whatever uniforms they wear. It means the entire transformation of our personal, professional and political life into something more consistent with our real situation as small, dependent, fugitive creatures; all sharing the same limitations. Wherever we find people whose spiritual life is robust and creative, we find this transformation has been effected; this price has been paid.

Prayer is our whole life towards God, our whole drive towards Him, humble correspondence of the human spirit with the Fountain of Life. This longing, this need of God, however dimly and vaguely felt, is the seed from which grows the strong, beautiful, fruitful plant of prayer. I find myself immersed in the modern world – subject to time, yet penetrated by the Eternal. To take up that double obligation to the seen and unseen, in however homely and practical a way, is to enter consciously upon the spiritual life.

*We must endure a mysterious pressure, which operates more often and purely in darkness than in light. This deeply grateful recognition of the Divine action is specially discovered in those disciples and sufferings which teach courage to the soul, distinguishing the truly awakened spirit. An uncalculating surrender, losing all individual preferences and reluctances in the vast outlines of God's mysterious design, is the condition. To make this willed surrender is the most solemn dignity of the human soul. The lesson of Christianity is what can be done with suffering, when it's met with self-oblivious courage and love. A certain slowing down and spacing out of our ceaseless clockwork activities is a necessary condition of the deepening. The spirit of Joy and the spirit of Hurry cannot live in the same house.

*The creative action of the Spirit penetrates the whole of life, and is felt by us in all sorts of ways. A genuine inner life must make us more and more sensitive to that moulding power, working upon

His creation at every level – especially the constant small but expert touches, felt in and through very homely events, upon those half-made, unsteady souls, the subject of His detailed care. The true splendour and heart-searching beauty of the Divine Charity is not seen in those cosmic energies that dazzle and confound us; but in the transcendent power that stoops to an intimate, cherishing love – the grave, steadfast Divine action, sometimes painful, sometimes gentle, on the small unfinished soul.

We're so busy rushing about. How little we know God's creative action, so hidden and penetrating. God knows the recipe He's working from and the result He wants to obtain. A generous acceptance of this ceaseless creative process, and willingness to be transformed in whatever way is wanted, at whatever cost, unselfs the inner life, making it accessible to the searching, delicate action of God.

For discussion

- It's hard to see what God is doing in our lives, but can you think of ways He may have been working in yours over the past year?
- How might you become more alert to God's loving Presence day to day?
- What kinds of things (perhaps concerns, joys or interests) are currently getting in the way of you being more attentive to God's action?

Prayer

Father, please awaken me! Unblock my ears and open my eyes, so I become more aware of how You're constantly loving me and initiating things in my life. Please forgive me when I fail to recognise what You're doing. Only You, God, know me fully and You love me better than I can love myself. So please give me what I need, for I don't know what to ask. And help me offer myself wholly to You, in Jesus' name, Amen.

5

Father, hallowed be Your Name

If Advent is about awakening to God's Eternal Action – around us and within us – our natural response after encountering God will be to worship. Christ taught us in the Lord's Prayer to recognise our privileged relationship with the God who is our Father. So our prayers open not with petition but with praise and adoration as we seek to enter into the deepest meaning of much-loved and familiar words. Evelyn reminds us that self-interest dries up adoration and we need to guard against the poison of 'spiritual egoism'.[1] Co-operating with the Spirit's work of cleansing and refreshing us will help us get ourselves out of the way so we can truly worship God.

> In . . . adoring prayer, the soul is . . . carried into God, hidden in Him. This is the only way in which it can achieve that utter self-forgetfulness . . . we gradually and imperceptibly learn more about God by this persistent attitude of humble adoration, than we can hope to do by any amount of mental exploration. Our soul recaptures, if only for a moment, the fundamental relation of the tiny created spirit with its Eternal Source. The time is well spent getting this relation and keeping it right. In it we breathe deeply the atmosphere of Eternity . . . We realise, and re-realise, our tininess, our nothingness, and the greatness and steadfastness of God. If you have only as little as half an hour to give each morning to your private prayer . . . spend half that time in such adoration . . . its neglect is responsible for much lack of spiritual depth . . . We must become, and keep, spiritually fit.[2]

For GOD is great . . . His furious beauty . . . royal splendour radiates from Him, a powerful beauty sets Him apart . . . Bow before the beauty of GOD, then to your knees – everyone worship!
(Psalm 96.4–6, 8–9, MSG)

God . . . holds me together . . . God delivers generous love . . . The deeper Your love, the higher it goes; every cloud is a flag to Your faithfulness. Soar high in the skies, O God! Cover the whole earth with Your glory!
(Psalm 57.2–3, 10, 11, MSG)

*The first movement of Christian prayer is the Glory of the Father. In those rare glimpses of Christ's life of prayer, we notice perpetual reference to the unseen Father; so much more vividly present to Him than anything that's seen – that strong, tranquil Presence – childlike trust must govern our relation to the Unseen. 'You are of God, little children' (1 John 4.4, NKJV). Were this the constant attitude of our spirits, our whole life – inward and outward – would be transformed. For we're addressing One who's already there, in charge of the situation.

The prevenience of God is the dominant fact of all life, of prayer. We open the doors of our hearts – direct our fluctuating wills to a completely present Love and Will moulding us. One meaning of Christ's incarnate life is to show us how to love this Present God; who comes to us in this thing and that thing, yet induces in us a thirst and longing that can't be satisfied by anything but Himself. The praying soul accepts its true status as a member of the whole family of humanity, accepting as a corollary of our filial relation with God, a brotherly, sisterly relation with all other souls, however diverse – replacing 'mine' by 'ours'.

God has created our craving for Himself alone. Even the brief flashes of Eternity which sometimes visit us make all else seem lifeless – unreal. There shouldn't be any situation, attitude, pre-occupation or relationship, from which we can't look up to God and say, 'Our Father'. Our inheritance *is* God, our Father and Home. We recognise Him, because we already carry in our hearts a rough sketch of His beloved countenance. Looking into those deeps, as into a quiet pool in a dark forest, we there find looking back at us the Face we implicitly long for and already know.[3] It's set in another world, another light: yet it's here. As we realise this, our prayer widens until it embraces the extremes of awestruck adoration and confident love – fusing them into one.

'Hallowed be Your Name' – adoration of God. This, says our Lord, is the way that you must begin, because it's the essence of religion. Since the Nature and Name of God is Love, this means a deep reverence for love in all its manifestations. Love is always to be recognised and adored, for it's God's signature lying upon creation; often smudged and faded, almost blotted out, yet legible to eyes cleansed by prayer. The saints can read the letters of the Name wherever found, whatever script; Francis read them on the face of the Crucified, in the leper's marred features and written in the air by the moving wings of free birds. 'Faith sees in everything the action of God.'[4]

The reason for the Church's existence is the more perfect hallowing of the Name; for the Church is the Body in and through which the Son utters the Father's praise. With one hand we touch the most secret intimacies of the Spirit, our loving, childlike relation to God; with the other, the creature's unlimited awe before His mystery – growing deeper, the nearer we approach.

Our prayer must always bring a dim yet certain sense of the Godhead's secret life over against us, which kills cheap, familiar sentimentalisms. It's those who see much who realise how much remains unseen. That's why theologians always have plenty to say about God; while the contemplative can hardly say anything at all. The fluent teacher, with sharp outlines and neat lists of attributes, is only the person with the telescope, not the Alpine guide. Real prayer is an entering into ignorance. A timid, upward gaze towards the splendour which baffles the mind, while satisfying the heart. Confronted by utter abasement of the creature before the Holy, this awestruck hallowing of the Name must be the first response of the praying soul.

Our Father in Heaven, hallowed, revered, be Your mysterious Name in my dim, fluctuating soul, to which You've revealed Yourself in such a degree as I can endure. May all my contacts, relationships, struggles, temptations, thoughts, dreams and desires be coloured by this loving reverence. Let me ever look through and beyond circumstance to You, so all I am and do may become more worthy of God, the origin of all. May that Name, too, be hallowed in my work, keeping me in remembrance that You are the doer of all that's really done: my part is that of a humble collaborator, giving my best.

This means that adoration, a delighted recognition of God's Life and Action, subordinating everything to the Presence of the Holy, is the essential preparation for action. That stops all feverish strain, rebellion, despondency, sense of our importance, worry about our success; and gives dignity, detachment and tranquillity to our action, and may make it of use to Him – cleansing from egoism, orienting towards God, reminding us our life and work are insignificant, except in so far as they glorify God.

Our response to each experience God puts in our path, from the greatest disclosure of beauty to the smallest appeal to love, from perfect happiness to utmost grief, will either hallow or not hallow His Name; this is the only thing that matters. The rest of the Lord's Prayer is about the different ways this adoring response can be made more complete; for it asks for the sanctification of everything that exists – the mouse's tail and seraph's wing, transfigured by God's radiance. All creatures taking part in the one great utterance of the Name: all self-interested striving transformed into this one great striving for God's glory. The whole life of Heaven and earth standing in adoration before the Lord and Giver of its life. All must be brought to the altar – consecrated to the purposes of the Holy.

Wholehearted adoration is the only real preparation for right action: action which develops within the Divine atmosphere, in harmony with God's Eternal Purposes. The Bible is full of illustrations of this truth, from the call of Isaiah to the Annunciation. First the awestruck recognition of God, then the doing of His Will. We can't discern His Eternal Purpose, even as it affects our tiny lives, opportunities and choices, except with the eyes of disinterested, worshipping love.

For discussion

- What resonated with you in this excerpt? Why do you think you were drawn to these thoughts?
- Reflecting on the way you pray, is adoration of God usually your starting point or do other concerns generally come first?
- Can you discern a link between the content of your prayers and the way you feel God may be working in your life?

Prayer

Loving God, You are my Father, my Papa, and I come to You in faith and loving expectancy. Draw me near and help me perceive how mysteriously You shower Your love upon me. May I be confident that You're looking after me and that You know what You're doing, even when I feel I've no idea what's going on! I praise You, my lovely Father God, and I'll worship You for ever and ever, Amen.

6

Your Kingdom come

Our prayer begins with recognition of God's ceaseless comings to us. Of course, God's Kingdom also comes into time through the particular in-breaking of the Incarnation: redemption will be complete only when the whole of creation is consecrated to God's Purposes, and enfolded in His serenity and love. The Church continues to pray for this.

But praying for the Kingdom to come is challenging! For we offer up not only creation but our own souls too. As Evelyn writes, the meaning of 'Your Kingdom come' is co-operation with God's redeeming, transforming action, whatever the cost.[1] As God's fellow workers, we're to help bring more of the Kingdom in – each faith-filled upward glance, movement of trust and selfless, loving act helps.[2] The 'real' Christian, according to Evelyn, will always be a 'revolutionary' – one who belongs to a 'new race', who is given a 'new name' and a 'new song'.[3] In this excerpt, Evelyn reflects upon the nature of God's Kingdom and how we might participate in its coming.

He made us in order to use us, and use us in the most profitable way; for His purpose, not ours . . . 'Thy Will be done – Thy Kingdom come!' There is energy, drive, purpose in those words . . . a total concentration on the total interests of God, which must be expressed in action . . . an eager willingness – to take our small place in the vast operations of His Spirit, instead of trying to run a poky little business on our own . . . trying to see things, persons and choices from the angle of Eternity.[4]

God's Word vaults across the skies from sunrise to sunset,
Melting ice, scorching deserts, warming hearts to faith. The
revelation of GOD is whole and pulls our lives together . . . Keep
me from stupid sins, from thinking I can take over Your work.
(Psalm 19.6–7, 13, MSG)

God's Kingdom is like an acorn that a farmer plants. It is quite
small as seeds go, but in the course of years it grows into a huge
oak tree, and eagles build nests in it . . . God's Kingdom is like
yeast that a woman works into the dough for dozens of loaves
of barley bread – and waits while the dough rises.
(Matthew 13.31–33, MSG)

*The Kingdom is God's serenity already enfolding us, seeking to
penetrate and redeem the whole created order. We pray for this
transformation, healing misery, violence, confusion and unrest,
through the Holy Spirit's coming – to enter, cleanse, sanctify –
one thing working in another, as leaven in our dough, to redeem
and rule. It's the constant prayer of the whole Church, voicing the
world's one need.

The world is saved by Incarnation. 'I came forth from the
Father, and am come into the world' (John 16.28, KJV). This perpetual advent is the coming into time of the Kingdom of Heaven:
Emmanuel, God with us. The whole creation is won from rebellion
and consecrated to Christ's creative purposes. His Spirit conquers
by penetration, entering by the open door of prayer, spreading to
entincture the whole of life. 'Our God shall come, and shall not
keep silence' (Psalm 50.3, KJV), but the coming will be very quiet.
Without observation, the Eternal slides into the successive by inconspicuous paths, transforming to its purpose; the humble birth
in a crowded stableyard, the love's victory when a young prophet
gave Himself to the Father's purpose on the Cross. The action
of God is seldom showy; the true energies of the Kingdom are

supersensuous – only a little filters through to the visible world. More and more we must expect our small action to be overruled and swallowed up in the vast Divine action; ready to offer it to fulfil God's purpose, however much this differs from ours.

The Christian turns again from the bewildered contemplation of history where God's so easily lost, to the prayer of filial trust where He's always found; knowing that things which seem to turn to humanity's disadvantage may work to the Divine advantage. On the frontier between prayer and history stands the Cross, a perpetual reminder of the price by which the Kingdom is brought in. We live in illusion till that wisdom has touched us – the first coming of the Kingdom to individual souls.

It's great when any soul says without reserve, 'Your Kingdom come!' – acknowledging our present alienation, egoism and impurity, casting down the will, destroying our small, natural sovereignty; the risk and adventure accompanying unconditional submission to God, and total acceptance of the rule of Love. None can guess beforehand with what anguish, what tearing of old hard tissues and habits, the Kingdom will force a path into the soul, confronting self-love with God's penetrating demand. We can't use the words unless we're prepared to pay this price. Handing ourselves over to God that His Purposes, declared or secret, natural or spiritual, may be fulfilled through us and in us, and all that's hostile to His Kingdom done away.

There are two sides to this. The passive side means enduring, indeed welcoming, the inexorable pressure of God's transforming power in our lives; for the Kingdom comes upon earth bit by bit, as first one soul, then another is subjugated by love, and so redeemed. It means enduring the burning glance of the Holy upon imperfection, hardness, sin. The active side means self-offering for the Kingdom's purposes, in this visible world of space and time; the whole drive of our life, all our natural endowments, set towards a furtherance of God's Purposes – wide-spreading love transfiguring our use of money, time, position. Each act of love, sacrifice, conquest of prejudice and generous impulse carried through into action counts: and each unloving gesture, hard judgment, pessimistic thought or utterance, opposing the coming of the Kingdom, falsifies the life of prayer.

The Coming of the Kingdom is perpetual. Again and again freshness, novelty, power from beyond the world, breaks in by unexpected paths, bringing unexpected change. Those who cling to tradition, fearing all novelty in God's relation with His world, deny the Holy Spirit's creative activity. In the Church, this fresh invasion of God must constantly be repeated to escape the ever-present danger of stagnation. The Church is not a static institution but the living Body of the living Christ – the nucleus of the Kingdom in this world.

Yet the coming of the Kingdom means something deep, subtle and costly: the reign of God, the all-demanding and all-loving in individual hearts, overruling all the adverse powers that dominate human life. It means reordering, quieting our turbulent interior life, conquest of our rampant individualism by God's supernatural action; and that same supernatural action gradually making each human life what it's meant to be – a living part of the Body of Christ, a sacramental disclosure of God's Splendour.

To look with real desire for the coming of the Kingdom means crossing over to God's side; dedicating our powers to the triumph of His Purpose. The praying spirit accepts its most sacred privilege: active, costly co-operation with God – first its own purification, then His creative, redeeming action. Our attitude must be wide open towards God, exhibiting quite simply our poverty and impurity, acknowledging our second-rateness, but still offering ourselves as we are.

If we consider Christ's action as He moves declaring the Kingdom of God, we see Him bringing God's redeeming action into the texture of people's lives. He's singularly uninterested in lofty ideas and large projects, but greatly interested in redemptive acts. Christ announced the only purpose of His ministry to be bringing in God's Kingdom; by His quiet action of flawless love giving back to our lost, tormented planet its place in the orchestra of Heaven. Yet the way Christ spoke of this Kingdom was always allusive, suggestive, poetic – never precise. The Mystery of the Kingdom is sacred and must be reverenced, not reduced to a formula. Instead of definition, we're given a series of vivid contrasting pictures of some of the things that it's like. Its inconspicuousness yet tremendous latent energy – like seed that has in itself the whole life of the tree: like leaven working unseen the transformation of the dough. Its overwhelming attraction for those who recognise it – the Pearl, the Treasure.

Again, the Kingdom is present already, mingling disguised with the untransformed, common life; and sometimes the form in which it meets us has no beauty. It's recognised by its fruits. It enters the world by the action of One who sows. God's wheat and the devil's darnel, which looks at first glance like wheat, grow together. Real and sham charity; the real Christian and self-occupied devotee. The hurried enthusiast, the keen reformer, eager to apply absolute standards, wants to pull up the darnel and leave the wheat. But God's wise tolerance leaves both growing together; content that the genuine crop be known by its yield.

For discussion

- The Kingdom of God is constantly breaking into our world. How conscious are you of little signs of the Kingdom and how might you become more aware of these?
- Evelyn mentions a passive and an active side of being involved in bringing in God's Kingdom. How do you feel you are participating?
- You might make a deliberate choice today to try to 'see things, persons and choices from the angle of Eternity', and then consider, what difference has this made to my response?

Prayer

O Lord, You set before us the great hope that Your kingdom will come on earth, and You teach us to pray for its coming. There are already many signs of its dawning! Please give me eyes to see these and grace to participate in its fuller coming, as I pray and work for that day when Your Will shall be done on earth, as it is in Heaven, through Jesus Christ our Lord, Amen.

Part 2

ADVENT: AWAITING GOD'S COMING (CHRIST IS COMING)

We move from Part 1, where our focus was God, to Part 2, Advent. God has come to us in creation, and now we wait, with expectant longing, for His coming in the person of Christ.

7

Advent waiting

Mary is our archetype for Advent as we watch and wait. Her capacity for God – 'full of grace' as emptied of self – enables her to play her part in our Lord's coming. It's only as we follow her example and offer our lives humbly to God that we may become a 'pure capacity' for Him and a channel for His love to others.[1]

In the silence of Advent waiting, we can attend to God, and, like Mary in her pregnancy, we will find ourselves enlarged in the waiting. Evelyn wrote in her personal journal that her life was too fast and packed with events and noise, adding that she would never improve in prayer and vision unless she had stretches of quiet.[2] We all know what it's like to be carried away by the world's craving for haste and immediate results. In these short excerpts, Evelyn encourages us not to be hurried or harried but to develop a leisured attentiveness, training ourselves to feel God's gentle pressure and hear His Voice.[3] A balance between surrendered waiting and action is what's needed. And as we find ourselves becoming more sensitive to the music of God, and more responsive to Him, our self-giving to others will be enriched.

We are spiritual creatures with the power of communion with God, breathing the air of Eternity. We can't keep this power unless we exercise it. Nor can we fully get it unless we train ourselves to it. We must accustom our attention, that wanders over all other interests, to fix itself on Him. Such deliberate attention to God is the beginning of real prayer.[4]

I pray to GOD – my life a prayer – and wait for what He'll say and do ... waiting and watching till morning.
(Psalm 130.5–6, MSG)

Mary: 'Behold the maidservant of the Lord! Let it be to me according to Your word.' (Luke 1.38, NKJV)

*The Blessed Virgin Mary stands for simple human nature as it ought to be – a pure capacity for God: full of grace because emptied of self: and so she's the classical pattern of every human soul turned to Him, whether the special vocation of that soul is prayer or service – homely, quiet self-sacrifice or great initiative. What matters is simply our capacity for God and our self-oblivious response. The true work of prayer, self-conquest and suffering, is to increase our latent capacity for God and so make us more useful to Him. 'Behold the handmaid of the Lord: be it unto me according to Your word': body and soul at the disposal of the Spirit.

*Withdraw from the restless surface of life in order to give our whole attention to the deeps of life: cut off relations with our visible environment, which generally obsesses us, in order to realise better our invisible environment – God – and adjust ourselves better to Him, His demands, His gifts. Hear the whisper and see the light that comes to us from beyond the world and shows us how to live. The longer we go on with life, the more mysterious it seems to us. We go muddling on, knowing we are making a hash of it; people tell us this and that, but somehow they all seem rather like guesses in the dark. Only the Author of human life can really teach us to live human life. He alone knows what it's meant to be. And the only way to lay hold of this secret, or to recapture it, is to come to God and be alone with Him.

*Thousands of devoted men and women believe that the really good part is to keep busy – such a lot of urgent jobs for Martha to do. The result of this can only be a maiming of their human nature, exhaustion, loss of depth and vision; and it's seen in the vagueness and ineffectuality of a great deal of the work that is done for

God, nowhere more deadly than in the religious sphere – developing a lopsided Christianity; so concentrated on service, and on this-world obligations, as to forget the need of constant willed and quiet contact with that other world. Our inward growth conditions both our communion with God and our power of healing others. We see this double strain in all the best helpers of humanity. An alert sensitiveness to the Presence of God kept pace with outward deeds. Remember Elizabeth Fry, balancing her marvellous regenerative work by silent worship. Penitence kept pace with love, and prayer with work. Conscious loving dependence on greater sources of power. Our Lord's own teaching and works of power and mercy appear closely dependent on the nights He spent on the mountain in prayer.

We must replace material by spiritual values – the desire for goods by the desire for good, the desire for luxury by the desire for justice; quantity by quality; must dissolve acquisitiveness in that spirit of poverty.

*The thoughts of God are very deep. Bit by bit He moulds us to His image, by giving us some of His saving power, His redemptive love, and asking our co-operation. All our action must be peaceful, gentle and strong – depth and a steadiness which come from the fact that our small action is now part of the total action of God, whose Spirit 'works always in tranquillity'. Fuss, feverishness, anxiety, intensity, intolerance, instability, pessimism and wobble and every kind of hurry and worry – these, even on the higher levels, are signs of the self-made and self-acting soul; the spiritual parvenu. The saints know that they, and all the other souls they love so much, have their abiding place in Eternity; and there the meaning of everything that they do and bear is understood. So all their action comes from this centre; and whether it's small or great, heroic or very homely, doesn't matter to them much.

The action of those whose lives are given to the Spirit has in it something of the leisure of Eternity; and because of this, they achieve far more than those whose lives are enslaved by rush and hurry – the unceasing tick-tock of the world. Co-operation with the Spirit's action balances our communion with God, as a giving of ourselves to doing some of His work in the world. But there's another, deeper side: the hidden action of each soul called by God, the effort and struggle of the interior life – what we have to do in response to the Love that is drawing us out of darkness into His great light. Even that mysterious communion with God which we seek, and offer ourselves to, in spite of the deep peace it brings – is not without the pain and tension which must be felt by imperfect human creatures. Still more when it comes to the deeper action, the more entire self-giving, the secret transformation to which that vision of perfection calls us; and the sacrifice, struggle and effort which, sooner or later, this transformation must involve. 'You have made us for Yourself, and our hearts find no rest save in You.' But we must be willing to undertake the journey, whatever it costs. Many people suggest by their behaviour that God is of far less importance than their bath, morning paper or early cup of tea. The life of co-operation with Him must begin with a full, practical acceptance of the truth that God alone matters.

*The Church is a tool of God, not a comfortable, religious club. Every one of its members is required, in one way or another, to co-oper-ate with the Spirit in working for that great end: and much of this work will be done in secret, invisible ways. We are transmitters as well as receivers. Our contemplation and our action, our humble self-opening to God – keeping ourselves sensitive to His music and light – and our generous self-opening to our fellow creatures – keeping ourselves sensitive to their needs – ought to form one life; meditating between God and His world, and bringing the saving power of the Eternal into time. We are far from realising all that human spirits can do for one another on spiritual levels if they'll pay the price; how truly and really our souls interpenetrate, and how impossible and unchristian it is to 'keep ourselves to ourselves'.

For discussion

- What needs to change for you to be 'emptied of self' as Mary was so you can have a 'full capacity' for God?
- What might you cut out of your weekly activities so you have more time to attend to God in prayer?
- What distracts you when you try to wait for God in prayer, and what helps you stay attentive, patient and unhurried?

Prayer

Jesus, You communed with Your Father in solitary places, and told Your disciples to come apart and rest. Please give me the desire to linger with You in prayer, and refresh my soul through silence and solitude, so I may serve You with renewed energy and strength. Shift my gaze from myself so my eyes wait on You, O Lord – as those who wait for the morning. Let me look for You, dear Lord, and grant that I may both find You, and be found by You, in Jesus' name, Amen.

8

Advent expectancy

We speak of pregnancy as 'expecting' a baby. Pregnancy is permeated by a sense that, underneath the surface of our normal life with its daily rhythms, another life is growing that will change our world. There are some similarities with Advent: Evelyn encourages us to expect to see God actively doing things in the world, the Church, our communities and our lives. What makes this challenging is that God meets us in *unexpected* ways, perhaps humble, gentle, natural or obscure. Those awaiting the Messiah anticipated something large and showy: instead, the Incarnation was small, quiet and earthy – a baby born in poverty. Perhaps it's only as we expect the unexpected that we'll wake up enough to notice that God – *Emmanuel* – is truly with us.

This kind of expectancy is essential to our lives of prayer, for the Kingdom of God constantly surprises us. The Jews were envisaging a Messianic King but got a rabbi marked by compassionate self-oblivion, who was ready to accept suffering and even death. Often a school-nativity-play kind of enchantment can distract us from the reality of Advent, which calls us to show kindness towards our fellow human beings, sick and sinful as they (and we) may be.

Humanity, said Christ, is nourished by every word that proceeds out of the mouth of God. Not the words we expect, or persuade ourselves that we have heard; but those unexpected words He really utters, sometimes by the mouths of the most unsuitable people, sometimes through apparently unspiritual events, sometimes secretly within the soul.[1]

I'm leaping and singing in the circle of Your love; You saw my pain . . . You didn't leave me in their clutches but gave me room to breathe . . . Don't give up. Expect GOD to get here soon.
(Psalm 31.7–8, 24, MSG)

This resurrection life you received from God is not a timid, grave-tending life. It's adventurously expectant, greeting God with a childlike 'What's next, Papa?'
(Romans 8.15, MSG)

*Advent is a time of expectation, an eager looking out of the natural creature towards the spiritual world. It's a looking out to something that's going to come to us just because we so long for its advent and can't get it of ourselves. Redemption is set going in the most natural of ways. Remember what's said in the New Testament about those expecting the Kingdom of God? What did they expect? They'd been fed on apocalyptic literature – fluffy, heady stuff. And what they got was just a poor person's baby born under the most unfortunate circumstances. In Christ's infancy, instant recognition of the true reality broke out at every level: angels, shepherds, wise men. We only realise it, in all its poignancy, when we become little children too.

There's always the naturalness of the supernatural, the fact that the name *Emmanuel* means what it says: 'God with us'. God gives through nature all the necessities that matter for the transfiguring of the soul. His redemptive energy is most perfectly manifested through human beings. This truth is revealed in the gentlest, humblest way, right down through history, in homely surroundings. A carpenter's baby. Thirty years of obscure village life. Self-identification with the crowd. The refusal of all self-regarding use of spiritual power. Immense compassion. A self-oblivion so perfect we don't notice it. A genial love of all human and natural things. Unflinching acceptance of suffering, failure and death. Together these were the chief external signs of God's full expression in terms of human personality. If it hadn't happened, we should never have invented it like that. Our highest values couldn't have come to us in a humbler disguise. This is a reverse of our ordinary human standards, a reverse so crushing, so complete. It reminds us that the real Incarnation is a bit of uncompromising Divine realism, not a lovely mystery play.

It's easy to enjoy Christmas with its live altar as a crib, clean straw, nice furry animals and its Christmas-card atmosphere of sweetness and charm. In the same way, it was easy for the Jews in Christ's time to enjoy Temple worship with the Holy of Holies, Ark and Veil: all this undying appeal stimulates and enchants us. But redemption wasn't worked out in Temple worship. It was worked out in ordinary life among the ruck of the sinful, sick, maimed, stupid and self-interested. It was accomplished through sharing the suffering and injustice of life. There was a Temple ritual all ready, but Reality reached and won its creatures by contact through personality, a contact that then and now evades nothing and leaves nothing out.

'This really *is* the Messiah!' We see that transcendent human soul knowing its power, yet choosing compassion instead of ambition – human courage and generosity blazing out in the shadow of death, the human agony and self-abandonment of Christ. Here is the Supernatural, God, seeking us through natural means and known character. His direct action on the human being is through a human being. His demand on souls is to be so completely surrendered, that through them, His love and holiness can be expressed. Doesn't Christ's life of human compassionate service supported by lonely prayer give us a pattern of humble growth? Isn't it a pattern on which all Christians must keep their eyes as they seek to imitate it in thousands of degrees and ways?

The saints, as they drew near to God, tried to imitate that pattern more and more closely, and as they did so, their personalities expanded and shone with love and power. Especially in its most mysterious reaches, in redemptive action on suffering and sin, the saints dimly reproduced and continue to reproduce Christ's life. When we're fully awake in our souls, we *can* accept redemptive suffering for one another.

Real redeeming saints look to the outsider more like a publican (a tax collector) than a Pharisee, being so abased and self-identified with sinners. Such people don't stand aside, feeling pure and agreeable to God, but go right down into the mess and acknowledge their part in it. The edges of the mess are melted off and saints are now fused with the world which they love and want to help. Such people know that we come from God, belong to God and are destined for God!

That seems far beyond us, yet perhaps there are ways we too can seek to incarnate love such as this. As Advent shows us, expectation itself is an implicit knowledge of God and a condition of prayer. So too is the trustful craving of the soul for holiness and grace. In the interior life, there's often more sanctifying power in such humble waiting on God than in its vivid realisation. The dull shutting of our gates on fresh possibilities thwarts God's action and only contradicts each individual act of faith and self-abandonment. Peaceful self-yielding to the Spirit opens more and more of the gates for God's entrance into the human soul, which in welcome cries, 'Behold, the handmaid of the Lord!'

It's not hard for most of us to do active work, but it's hard to maintain that spirit of unflickering self-renunciation and waiting. Yet the Incarnation has taught, and through the saints goes on teaching, that what matters is not what we do, but is the deepness and self-abnegation with which we enter the life, movement and will of God, and so can be used for Divine Purpose. Not the things that Christ did but His attitude and intention compel our response. We must get rid of the pestilent, deadly notion that the amount of things we get through is the standard. The steadiness with which we radiate God is the standard. Christ did this at dinner parties, on journeys, with friends and through healing and preaching. This transfiguration of the ordinary shows us God in the flesh, and it's always this that wins souls. Real saints are continuing the work of incarnation through the perfect self-yielding of the soul to God, making themselves His tools, His channels of revelation to others. They show us little sudden hints of the wonderful fact of Eternal Love ever at work in human history, patient with human perversions, endlessly compassionate to human loneliness and sin, gradually penetrating and sanctifying human life – entering, transforming and enlarging the capacity of human character, and making us fellow workers with God.

For discussion

- What are some of the unexpected ways God has met you in the past, and where do you think God may long to meet you now?
- What practical things might you do to nurture a greater expectancy of God's Presence this Advent?
- Can you think of someone you know who steadily radiates God to others?

Prayer

Lord, I confess I'm so distracted by the busyness of every day that I scarcely expect You to meet me. Give me courage to welcome You, even before I fully discern and recognise You, whatever Your disguise. Help me to look for Your coming and expect Your loving Presence and initiative in my small life, and give me Your very self, in Jesus' name, Amen.

9

Advent hope

Hope, which we might define as a certainty of God's goodness, is the attitude that underlies our Advent waiting. It's Mary's hope that enables her to meet her unusual destiny with poise and a lack of self-concern. And nowhere is hope more powerfully demonstrated, argues Evelyn, than on Good Friday, when Christ abandons Himself to the sacrificial suffering of the Cross – sure that, despite appearances, God's loving Purposes will prevail. Hope helps us cope with the baffling messiness of life because we trust that God is always for us and that's what really matters. Of course, journeying on in hope is not easy! It takes courage: but we can find strength in the promise that one day all that has so confused us will become clear, and we will finally see our Lord – face to face.

Hope is a completely confident expectation; that sureness and certitude with which the awakened soul aims at God and rests in God. It is the source of that living peace; that zest and alertness, that power of carrying on, which gives its special colour to the genuine Christian life . . . people speak much of Easter Hope; but it's surely the Good Friday hope, with its lesson of self-oblivious confidence in life's blackest moments, that speaks most clearly to our needs . . . By that contemplation we're lifted from all petty preoccupation with our own reasons for despondency, taught to look on wide horizons, confident that in suffering and apparent failure we contribute to the mysterious purposes of the God we love.[1]

I've cultivated a quiet heart. Like a baby content in its mother's arms, my soul is a baby content. Wait, Israel, for GOD. Wait with hope. Hope now; hope always!
(Psalm 131.2–3, MSG)

Let us hold unswervingly to the hope we profess, for He who promised is faithful.
(Hebrews 10.23, NIV)

*Hope lifts our experience into the Eternal Light, saying, 'Even though I don't see the meaning, I know all this is conditioning my growth, purifying my spirit, taking me towards You; and nothing matters but that.'

Hope finds all life penetrated by a significance that points beyond itself, and has a trustful expectation that the ceaseless stream of events, thoughts, joys, trials – the whole stuff of experience – means something, points beyond itself to God. Such Hope is the bright side of self-abandonment – merging the interests of that little life in the vast interests of the Divine Love and Will. Think about that mysterious, living Love pressing in on human history, and here and there working through the shimmer of holiness, the sharp glint of sacrifice. I will forget my personal discomfort, unsteadiness and anxieties and anchor myself there. It's true that my little boat rolls heavily on the surface of the waves, and often makes me feel very ill; but under those waves is the firm ground of the Life of God. This sense that beyond all appearance we depend utterly on the Goodness of God, and can depend on it – this is Hope. Such Hope gives the spiritual life its staying power.

The whole of Christian history really turns upon the power of human hope: this absolute hold upon the reality of God, His supernatural energy and freedom, with the corresponding conviction that He does and will act within the human arena, intervene to save. 'I am not a God afar off: I am your Maker and friend' (Jeremiah 23.23) – a Maker who hasn't finished His work, but is making us all the time, whose capacity for loving action is inexhaustible.

The psychological landscape in which the greatest event in humanity's spiritual history was prepared, was coloured by Expectation, Hope. Christ was born among those who waited for the consolation of Israel; who were sure, in spite of baffling appearance, that the Purpose of God would be fulfilled. The Blessed Virgin, standing at the budding-point of Christian history, meets her strange destiny with selfless confidence. The same necessary condition runs through the Gospels. If we ask we get, if we seek we find, if we knock hopefully on the door, it will open. The unlimited world of Eternal Life is here on the threshold with its riches; it's for us to stretch out to it with confidence. The Spirit of God works in and with the faithful hopeful will that expects, and waits upon, the supernatural response.

In the events of Holy Week, Jesus teaches by demonstration the lesson of an unconquerable Hope; the anchoring of the soul's trust, beyond all appearance, in the infinite Life of God. From the poor, little triumph of Palm Sunday, to the agony of Gethsemane and Calvary – with an ever-increasing sense of isolation, forsakenness and darkness, culminating in the utter helplessness and ignominy of the Cross. The soul of Christ moves with a steadiness, transcending human agony, sure that, in spite of appearances, the Will of God is holy, and that along these dark paths, by utmost sacrifice and apparent failure, the Purposes of His Love must prevail. That supernatural Hope transfigured even the awful moment of dereliction when He felt Himself abandoned by God – tasted the horrors of spiritual death. Through this darkness, Jesus rose to the heights of self-abandoned trust. 'Father, into Your hands I commend My Spirit' – the evening prayer of every Jewish child; 'I don't ask, know or guess, what's going to happen; You are my Hope!'

The cleansing touch is already completely present in all the ups and downs, trials, sacrifices, humiliations of our personal and professional life; in all those inequalities of health, affection, opportunity, which mortify self-will and self-esteem. It's the business of Hope, tending here and now to God, to recognise within these baffling accidents the operations of Creative Love, and its own duty of collaboration; looking fairly and squarely at all that needs to be done to fit the soul for its destiny, and then starting the work in perfect confidence that the energy of God is with us from the moment that we really take the scrubbing-brush into our hands.

He has made us for Himself; but the fulfilment of that Hope is partly in our own hands. It requires our generous, courageous response to the secret Divine incentive, our peaceful acceptance of purification, our active love. There's one fragment of the Eternal Purpose which no one else can fulfil, one place in the world where we and none other are meant to transmit God's Life and Love, and so fulfil His Hope. Even in our timid souls there's born a faint desire to give ourselves without reserve to His Purpose, whatever the cost. There's work that God requires to be done by each one of us, which no one else can do. Therefore our business is to get down to it, checking the instinctive recoil of the inferiority complex, the easy resort to 'I'm not up to it: there must be some mistake'. Hope means taking risks – entering upon a path of which we do not see the end. It believes in the God of the future, as well as the past. It knows how to combine a living suppleness and freedom with an utter self-abandonment, a humble self-knowledge with a vigorous initiative.

Our Lord found great significance in the life of birds; in their freedom, their self-abandoned trust, their release from mere carefulness. He held them precious to God, and as patterns for the faith and hope of humanity. I sometimes think that the Divine Gift of Hope – that confident tendency of the soul, that trust in the Invisible, and in a Country, truly awaiting us; poured into humanity by God to give meaning and buoyancy to their life – all this was first, as it were, tried out in the birds – giving themselves trustfully to the supportive air. Hope is Love, tending to God at all costs.

For discussion

- Does this excerpt change your perception of the challenges in your life at present? If so, in what ways?
- What do you hope for?
- When does it feel difficult to trust God and have hope?

Prayer

Lord, You are love and You love me. Fill me with hope and encourage me to expect You to be constantly generous! Thank You that You're such a faithful God and help me to hope in You and trust Your ongoing care. When I experience confusion and fear and pain, may I rest in You, knowing all things are safe in Your hands. Grant me, as You've promised, peace that passes understanding so I can face the clouds and the darkness, knowing darkness and light are both alike to You, through Jesus Christ our Lord, Amen.

10

Advent silence

We've been reflecting on how Advent is a season of waiting, expectancy and hope, with God at work in mysterious ways. It's a time to cultivate an inner stillness so we may attend to what we usually miss amid the busyness of the Christmas season. God comes softly, for we couldn't bear it if He didn't speak to us tenderly. We may not hear Him if other voices compete, so we're encouraged to take ourselves to a quiet place to pray, leaving our phones, laptops and the noisy world that makes our need for silence paramount. There is a huge difference between deep prayer and distracted prayer; deliberately immersing ourselves in silence to attend to God will help us keep our spiritual poise, and after a while we may well catch notes of the music of Eternity.[1]

> Mechanical silence, the silence for which one struggles, is one of the most sterile of silences . . . But if each person attends to God in the way we attend to anyone we deeply love . . . the result will be all right . . . phrases of aspiration . . . quiet us, but they stir us to feel the love, humility, and adoration which they suggest.[2]

> Silence is praise to You, Zion-dwelling God, And also obedience. You hear the prayer in it all.
> (Psalm 65.1–2, MSG)

> Keep your mouth shut, and let your heart do the talking.
> (Psalm 4.4, MSG)

*We enter the silence – readjust our balance, attend to all we usually leave out, get away from distractions of talking and action. We sink into our souls where God's voice is heard. Without silence around us, the inward stillness in which God educates and moulds us is impossible. We come to rest before God, to find space for recollection, in which we possess our souls and learn His Will.

It's an *elected silence*. We have, for our examples, Enoch, who silently listened for God's voice to discern the Divine Will, and Teresa, quiet and alone in her watchtower. Remember, silence is more than non-talking. It's a complete change in the way we use our minds. We lead very active lives. Our mental machinery is made so the more active our work, the more incessant the whirr of wheels, the harder it is to be quiet in the Divine Presence. Yet *nothing* so improves that active work as such quietude, the sense of Eternity and restful reception of the Holy Spirit, ceasing introspection and altruistic fidgets. Only in such silence can we look out of our workshop window and see the horizons of the spiritual world.

Our deepest contacts with God are so gentle because they're all we can bear. We need quiet to experience them. They don't come as an earthquake of mental upheaval or in the scorching fire or rushing wind of emotion. In the silence, there's nothing devastating or sensational, but only a still, small voice. To be silent with nature is to witness to God.

Your objective is to attend to God, to Christ, to learn His Love and what He wants of you, for facing realities in His Light, for thinking in His Presence. It's an opportunity to be like the simple but devoted old man who was asked how he prayed, and quietly replied: 'We look at one another.' Make *that* your aim. We do it by forgetting ourselves.

There are two thoughts with which I suggest we live. First, the wonderful words of Christ in the High Priestly Prayer: 'For their sakes I sanctify myself' (John 17.19, KJV). Such an attitude is so deeply true, for it redeems personal religion from its self-regarding taint. Yet we can't give to anyone what we don't ourselves possess. It's impossible to bring Christ to others until He's been revealed *in* us, as Paul said (Galatians 1.15–16). That's a solitary experience. The more we deepen our lives in God, the more we surrender and learn to realise His Presence, the more use we'll be to those we serve. Don't we sometimes feel how thin and poverty-stricken our lives are? Therefore, for *their* sakes, we deepen our interior resources through prayer, adoration, joy and confidence in God. The more we love, the better is our work. But the sanctified outlook is hard to keep up. It's impossible without a vision of our work in God and the vision of His Spirit in us and in all others too. Our task as children of God is to grow more and more up into this.

*We come to be alone with God, attending to God, to recover our spiritual poise. We don't come for spiritual information, but for spiritual food and air – to wait on the Lord and renew our strength – not for our own sakes but for the sake of the world. 'When you pray, enter into your closet – and *shut the door*' (Matthew 6.6). I think we can almost see the smile with which Christ said those three words: and those three words can define what we have to try to do. Anyone can retire into a quiet place and have a thoroughly unquiet time in it. It's the shutting of the door that makes the whole difference. The voice of God is very gentle; we can't hear it if we let other voices compete. It's no use entering that closet, that inner sanctuary, clutching the daily paper, your engagement book and a large bundle of personal correspondence. All these must be left outside. God only, God in Himself, sought for Himself alone.

You would hardly enter the presence of the human being you most deeply respected and loved in the state of fuss, preoccupation and distraction in which we too often approach God. You are to 'centre down' into that deep stillness which is the proper atmosphere of your soul. Remain with God. Wait upon the Light. 'Commune with your Father which is in secret' (Matthew 6.6). There's always something dark and hidden. The closet where we speak to Him is not very well lit – but the light that filters into it is a ray of the Eternal Light on which we can't easily look: but as we get used to it, sun ourselves in its glow, we learn, as we can bear it, to see more and more – be content to dwell with God in that dim silence. Gaze at Him *darkly*, as the mystics say.

*'You have the words of Eternal Life' (John 6.68, NKJV). We come into the silence to hear those words again and tune ourselves up to what they say. God Himself can't explain to us our true life as He sees it in its reality, any more than we can explain its true life to the cat. He sees each one of us in relation to His Eternity, sees us as little things He's making for Himself. He sees us within a spiritual world, surrounded and conditioned by spiritual forces of which we know hardly anything at all, but which are infinitely more important and powerful than all the things we fancy matter a great deal. God can come to His human children and show our life to us as it ought to be – make us see what it can be if nothing happens to spoil His perfect work of art. 'In the beginning was the Word' (John 1.1, KJV) – God's self-expression. 'God . . . has . . . spoken to us by His Son' (Hebrews 1.1–2, NKJV). Listen to the secret whisper of the Spirit, look at Christ again, for the contemplation of Christ is the first part of Christianity. One will help the other, enrich the other – open up our souls, our spiritual ears and eyes to the beauty of the Mystery. If we look steadily and humbly at Christ's life, each time we look we shall find ourselves shrinking by contrast, and at last we shall be so small we shall become as little children. Nothing could be better than that!

For discussion

- Evelyn reminds us that silence and action are linked. As members of Christ's mystical body, the Church, we're part of the 'organism through which Christ continues to live in the world'.

How do you feel you might 'incarnate' something of Christ's generous spirit to other people?

- How easy or difficult do you find it is to shut yourself away to pray? Perhaps you long for those moments; perhaps you feel you lack time or privacy or struggle to let go of the stresses and strains of the day.
- Imagine God gazing at you with love, compassion and deep understanding. Could it be He's gently nudging you to reorder your life in some way?

Prayer

Lord, quieten my busy thoughts so my soul may rest in silence in the stillness of Your Presence. Draw me close to You in that deep, simple prayer which says nothing yet communicates everything. All I desire to know or love is in You alone. Place me where You will; give or take from me what You will. I surrender myself to You, in Jesus' name, Amen.

11

Advent prayer

Out of the attentive stillness we've been keeping, our response will flow. It may be vocal, involving speaking to God, reciting the liturgy or praying the Psalms. Articulating truths out loud is an important part of Advent waiting, for grief and lament need to be expressed. We may find when we voice the Psalms, for example, that we are taken beyond our pain so we can praise God once more. Evelyn believed some vocal prayer should be part of the daily rhythm of prayer; it provides discipline and shape and leads us on to slower, quieter, deeper stages. When we're distracted, we may find set prayers invaluable.

A second form of prayer, meditation, was described by Evelyn as thinking in God's Presence in a way that involves our whole being – mind, feelings, will, imagination and body. We might begin by reflecting on a spiritual text (a Bible passage or writings by the Saints), and spend time brooding over this before God. We don't need to try to engineer some type of meditative 'experience'; we can simply focus on God in adoration, surrendering ourselves anew to Him. Evelyn recognised that meditation upon the Christian 'mysteries' – 'chewing the cud' of the Gospels, as it were – provides nourishment and is an inexhaustible basis for prayer.[1]

> Prayer is nothing else but a devout intent directed towards Him . . . Augustine's great saying, 'Love, and do what you like', becomes more completely true . . . the soul's real progress is . . . towards the unspoilt, trustful, unsophisticated apprehension of the little child . . . In prayer, will and grace co-operate. Neither a limp abandonment to the supposed direction of the Spirit, nor a vigorous determination to wrestle with God on

our own account, will do . . . it's useless to endeavour by willed struggle to reach a level of prayer to which we're not yet impelled by grace. We can't by stretching ourselves add an inch to our stature: the result will be strain, not growth.[2]

thrill to GOD's Word . . . chew on Scripture day and night.
(Psalm 1.2, MSG)

God, the one and only – I'll wait as long as He says . . . He's . . . breathing room for my soul.
(Psalm 62.1–2, MSG)

*In vocal prayer we speak, not only to God, but also to ourselves – filling our minds with love, praise and humility. Psychology insists that the spoken word has more suggestive power, is more likely to reach and modify our deeper psychic levels, than any inarticulate thought; for the centres of speech are closely connected with the heart of our mental life. Therefore those who value the articulate recitation of litanies and Psalms are keeping closer to the facts of existence than those remaining in a state of prayer. Some vocal prayer should enter into the daily rule even of the most contemplative soul. It gives shape and discipline to our devotions, keeping us in touch with the great traditions of the Church. Vocal prayers, if we choose them well, can rouse our dormant spiritual sense, bringing us into God's Presence. Hilton says, 'Praying with your mouth gets and keeps fervour of devotion, and if a person ceases from saying, devotion vanishes away.' As the life of prayer begins to exert its full power, vocal prayers will gradually but steadily become slower and more pondered. The soul finds in their phrases more significance, is led on by these phrases to one's own petitions and aspirations. This means a drawing near to the next stage – meditation – the first degree of mental prayer, where we don't repeat set forms.

Meditation is a word that covers a considerable range of

devotional states. It's perhaps most simply defined as thinking in the Presence of God. And since our ordinary thoughts are scattered, seldom poised for long, real meditation requires, as its preliminary, recollection – a deliberate gathering of ourselves together, a retreat into our own soul. This is more easily done by a simple exercise of the imagination, a gentle turning to God, than by those ferocious efforts towards concentrating which some manuals advise, which often end by concentrating attention on the concentration itself.

For some, the slow reading of a Bible passage or the *Imitation of Christ* leads directly to a state of prayer; for others, a quiet dwelling on one of God's attributes is a gateway to adoration. Articulate speech is now left aside, but the ceaseless stream of inward discourse may persist, becoming a secret conversation with God; while others will be led to a quiet ruminating on spiritual things. Every real meditation involves three points: for our mind, will and feelings are all exercised in it. We think in some way of the subject of our meditation. We feel the emotion, whether love, penitence or joy, which it suggests to us. And, finally, the aim of all meditative prayer is a resolution, a renewal of our surrender to God: an act of the will. Practically every person who prays at all, and hasn't reached one of the stages of contemplative prayer, can meditate in a simple way if they choose to practise this art, and it's most fruitful, especially perhaps in the early stages of the spiritual life. Many souls remain in this type of prayer throughout their spiritual course. It gives ample scope for variety.

*Meditation may not be your 'line'. It's entirely a matter of temperament. Try this way. (1) Put yourself into some position so easy and natural to you that you don't *notice* your body: shut your eyes. (2) Represent to your mind some phrase, truth, dogma, event – e.g. a phrase of the Lord's Prayer, the Passion, the Nativity. Something that occurs naturally. Don't think about it, but keep it before you, turning it over as you might finger some precious possession. (3) Deliberately, by an act of will, shut yourself off from your senses. Don't attend to touch or hearing, till the external world seems unreal and far away. Still holding on to your idea, turn your attention *inwards*, allow yourself to sink, as it were, downwards and downwards, into profound silence and peace, the essence of the meditative state. More you can't do for yourself: if you get further, you'll do so automatically as a consequence of the above practice. It's the 'shutting off of the senses' and what Boehme calls 'stopping the wheel of the imagination and ceasing from self-thinking' that's hard at first. Don't try these things when you're tired – it's useless: and don't give up the form of prayer that comes naturally to you: don't be disheartened if it seems at first a barren, profitless performance. It's quite possible to obtain spiritual nourishment without being consciously aware of it!

*Meditation not only feeds but also disciplines the mind and soul; gradually training us to steady our attention upon spiritual things. It helps us conquer distractions and forms an essential prelude to that state of profound recollection where the soul dwells almost without effort on things of God. It's generally regarded as one of the principal elements in an ordered devotional life. Most people who've taken the trouble to learn it get their spiritual food largely by this deliberate exercise of brooding, loving thoughts; entering into, dwelling on, exploring and personally applying the deeds and words of Christ or the saints, or the fundamental conceptions of religion. There are people, however, who find they simply can't practise these formal, discursive meditations. Where this inability is genuine, and not a disguised laziness, it generally co-exists with a strong attraction to a more simple, formless communion with God; that loving, generalised attention sometimes called 'affective prayer' – 'the prayer which articulates nothing but expresses everything'. Those in whom this tendency is marked and persistent should yield to it, abandon their own efforts and move with docility towards that form of communion to which they feel drawn.

Distraction is really lack of attention; and lack of attention is really lack of interest. Vocal prayer, rightly used, is a valuable reminder of realities we always tend to forget. It captures our psychic machinery and directs it to a spiritual end, maintaining our attention in His Presence. Aspirations give the mind something to hold on to, quiet it, lull distracting thoughts and gradually train our mental life to run more in the channels they mark out. Such habits when formed – and the formation takes time – are for the busy worker an immense source of security and peace.

*Spiritual reading gives you a subject to attend to that helps control wandering thoughts. Take some point from your daily New Testament reading and, asking God for His Light, brood on it in His Presence till it leads you into acts of penitence, love and worship. Some people are more imaginative and others more logical in their ways of meditating. Each should follow their *attrait* and not try to force themselves into a particular method. Prayer should never be reduced to a system. It's essentially a living, personal relationship, which tends to become more personal, and also more simple, as one goes on.

For discussion
- Evelyn advocates praying the Psalms out aloud. Have you tried this form of prayer before and, if so, what was your experience?
- How helpful do you find more meditative types of prayer?
- We're all different and beloved. Which type of prayer do you find most nourishes your personal relationship with God?

Prayer
O God, I'm only real in so far as I'm in You and You're in me. Gather me in Your arms and lift me above my troublesome, repetitive thoughts so I may enjoy the serenity of Your Presence. Let me breathe deeply the breath of Eternity and rest in Your Love. Then when I return to the everyday, clothed in Your Peace, may I do and bear whatever pleases You, in Jesus' name, Amen.

12

Advent contemplation

In her spiritual journal, Evelyn spoke of moving beyond her 'choc-olate-cream period' of emotional fervour to a quiet 'deepening adoration and self-abandonment'.[1] At some stage, many of us begin to embrace more contemplative ways of praying and perhaps we feel we come to know God in ways we can't understand simply through our minds.[2] We may start with vocal prayer or meditation and then find ourselves led into inward silence. It's worth noting that silent forms of prayer tend to be 'given' and beyond our control.

Evelyn is robust on the subject of people who complain they 'can't meditate', arguing that rather than focus on their capacity for meditation, they should examine their capacity for suffering and love.[3] She believes our tendency to action generally obliterates our 'contemplative side of experience', and the result is 'feverishness, exhaustion and uncertainty of aim' – all characteristics of the 'over-driven' and 'underfed'.[4] We are encouraged then to set aside time for prayer and, regardless of how distracted we may be, simply to offer that time to God.[5] The following short excerpts about contempla-tion come primarily from letters Evelyn wrote to provide spiritual nurture.

> Contemplation of Christ . . . means entering by a deliberate, self-oblivious and humble attention into the tremendous mys-teries of His Life – mysteries which each give us some deep truth about the Life and Will of God and the power and voca-tion of a soul that is given to God . . . They will break up, into colours we can deal with, that white light of God's Holiness at which we cannot look.[6]

Silence is praise to You, Zion-dwelling God, And also obedience. You hear the prayer in it all . . . Dawn and dusk take turns calling, 'Come and worship' . . . Oh, let them sing!
(Psalm 65.1–2, 8, 13, MSG)

Open your mouth and taste, open your eyes and see – how good GOD is . . . His ears pick up every moan and groan . . . If your heart is broken, you'll find GOD right there.
(Psalm 34.8, 15, 18, MSG)

*By contemplative prayer, I just mean the sort of prayer that aims at God in and for Himself and not for any of His gifts whatever, and more and more profoundly rests in Him alone: what St Paul meant by being *rooted* and *grounded* (Ephesians 3.17, KJV). When I read those words, I always think of a forest tree – the vast unseen system of roots, and their power of silently absorbing food. On that profound and secret life the whole growth and stability of the tree depends. It is rooted and grounded in a hidden world.

*If we are to find and feel the Eternal, we must give time and place to it in our lives – a desperate modern need in too busy, hurried lives. Such recollection – a gathering up of our interior forces and retreat of consciousness to its 'ground' – is the preparation of all great endeavour. It's more productive of strength to spend that odd ten minutes in the morning in feeling and finding the Eternal, than in flicking through the newspaper. This will send us off to the day's work properly orientated, gathered together, recollected and really endowed with new power of dealing with each circumstance.

*As to making an act of recollection, I generally (1) make a definite act of the will to *attend* to it, (2) offer some short verbal prayer holding on tight to each word, and (3) go on direct from that, or sometimes without finishing it, to a sort of staring at God. Of course, very often

69

it doesn't come off at all; and when it does (3) may vary from a mere deliberate act of meditation to real passivity, which is entirely outside our own control and should never be deliberately struggled for. Try to do this for 10 to 15 minutes every morning at first, not for longer while it's an effort. Put aside a given point of time for attending exclusively to God – and then spend it as seems natural when it comes, not in striving for states but just being content to give yourself up to Him and 'be as you are'.

'Real inward silence is not achieved by any deliberate spiritual trick. It develops naturally; and most often from the full exercise of mental prayer, which is the child of properly practised vocal prayer. No one ought to set to work to practise such inward silence until they feel a strong impulse to do so. If we try such artificial methods, we probably drift into a mere quietistic reverie: and such reverie, though pleasant, has nothing in common with real contemplative prayer. All the great masters of prayer insist that humble surrender, not constant fervour, is the best index of the soul's goodwill. An old English mystic tells us not to be like 'greedy greyhounds' snatching at God's gifts, but to come gently and willingly to His outstretched hand and take what He gives us.

*The favourite aspiration of St Francis was, 'My God, my God, what are You and what am I?' Such aspirations, formed from memories of past reading and prayers, rise spontaneously into consciousness as the prayer proceeds; and those whose minds are richly stored with Scripture phrases and liturgic forms will seldom be at a loss for them. 'Press towards God with the sharp dart of your longing love and take no thought for words.' Intuition here begins to take the place of logical considerations. Affective thought as well as rational thought is taken up into the life of prayer, which now overflows its first boundaries and invades wider regions of the self. There are pauses, periods of deep silence, hushed communion, which the soul feels to be more and more fruitful. Here we're at the threshold of that progressive absorption which leads to the true contemplative state. Gradually one act of will, affection or aspiration comes more and more to dominate the whole prayer, say of half an hour's duration or more: and is used merely to true up that state of attention which is the very heart of prayer. When this condition is established, the soul has reached the degree which is sometimes called the Prayer of Simplicity – simple attention or active contemplation. It's thrown open with great love and desire to God, but in so simple a way that it cannot analyse its own experience. Its whole impulse is to wait on Him rather than to speak to Him. In the effort to describe this degree of prayer, the author of *The Cloud of Unknowing* said, 'God may well be loved, but not thought. Therefore I'll leave all I can think and take to my love that which I cannot think.'

It's a mistake to imagine that such prayer can be well developed and preserved, unless a certain care be given to its mental preparation. It's far better to enter it with some special thought of God, *some* distinct orientation of the will, than in the state of vague blankness characteristic of quietism; for this will merely encourage distraction and religious daydreams. The ultimate object of all prayer is greater efficiency for God, not the limp self-abandonment of quietism; therefore, as the soul approaches the passive degrees, a careful discrimination becomes necessary. The direction of the mystics is that we should enter on simple contemplation with 'a devout intent directed to God', and there is something very definite about that.

The use of the higher degrees of prayer does not and should not ever mean the total abandonment of the lower degrees. The healthiness of our spiritual life depends to a great extent on its suppleness, and on the variety which we are able to impart to it. Never be afraid of such variety. The mystics are insistent on this point – go up and down the ladder of love: sometimes speaking and sometimes listening, sometimes thinking and sometimes resting in the communion that is beyond thought and speech.

71

For discussion

- 'It's more productive of strength to spend that odd ten minutes in the morning in feeling and finding the Eternal, than in flicking through the newspaper.' How do you respond to this?
- Do you feel drawn to engage in contemplative prayer? What could you do without – or do less of – so you can set aside time to spend quietly in the Presence of God?
- Evelyn warns us about the possibility of drifting off in reveries of 'vague blankness'. What helps you remain focused on God during times of silent prayer in His Presence?

Prayer

Loving God, teach me to pray! Increase my longing to become more contemplative and come and pray in me. Enter my heart and take me into You. I long to withdraw from the transience of the world and rest in You, God, the Eternal. Show me the path to You and reveal more of who You are, so I can love You more, in Jesus' name, Amen.

Part 3

EMMANUEL: RECOGNISING GOD'S COMING (CHRIST COMES)

We move from Part 2 – waiting for the Christ-child, to Part 3 – Christ has come! In this section Evelyn invites us to gaze at the person of Christ afresh, to listen to Him and to the whisper of the Spirit. We see into the depths of the Father's heart of God through His Incarnate Son, but this Divine Gift contains much mystery. In contemplating Christ, we need to be humbly attentive, watching and listening for the 'intimations of Eternity' He reveals.[1] Gradually, as we awaken to the wonder of *who* Christ is, we will seek more and more to recognise Him and to welcome Him into our daily lives.

Part 7

EMMANUEL RECOGNISING GOD'S COMING (CHRIST COMES)

13

The Incarnate Christ

Finally, after much waiting, the Christ-child comes! Unexpectedly, His birth takes place in the poverty of a stable. (This strange juxtaposition of the humble and the glorious should give us pause to consider any preoccupation we may have with worldly sophistication; it is clear from Mary's simple self-abandonment that gentle acceptance and trust are all God desires.) From such inconspicuous beginnings God's Power is unleashed. The contrast between lowliness and transcendent glory is no accident but a 'clue' to the nature of the Incarnation. True to God's Divine method of hiding in humility, the link between the temporal and the Eternal can only be 'recognised by love'.[1] Christ's birth needs to take place in *us,* so we can radiate His Light in the darkness and shine His Love into a broken world.

> The Incarnation means that the Eternal God enters our common human life with all the energy of His creative love, to transform it, to exhibit to us its richness, its unguessed significance; speaking our language, and showing us His secret beauty on our own scale . . .[2]

> The mountains take one look at GOD and melt, melt like wax before earth's Lord. The heavens announce that He'll set everything right, And everyone will see it happen – glorious! (Psalm 97.5–6, MSG)

Going through a long line of prophets, God has been addressing our ancestors in different ways for centuries. Recently He

spoke to us directly through His Son . . . This Son perfectly mirrors God, and is stamped with God's nature.
(Hebrews 1.1–3, MSG)

The Word was first, the Word present to God, God present to the Word. The Word was God . . . The Word became flesh and blood, and moved into the neighbourhood. We saw the glory with our own eyes, the one-of-a-kind glory, like Father, like Son, Generous inside and out . . .
(John 1.1–2, 14, MSG)

*The eternal Incarnation of the Holy, self-given for the world, brings us to the mingled homeliness and mystery of the Christian revelation. 'God speaks in a Son', a baby Son. He speaks in our language and shows us His secret beauty on our scale. The Christmas Day Gospel takes us back to the mystery of the Divine Nature – 'In the beginning was the Word.' The depth and richness of His Being are entirely unknown to us. Yet God, who is Love right through – who loves and is wholly present where He loves – so loved the world as to desire to give the deepest secrets of His heart to *us*.

A baby, God manifest in the flesh. The stable, the manger, the straw; poverty, cold, darkness – these form the setting of the Divine Gift. In this Child, God gives His supreme message to the soul – Spirit to spirit – but in a human way. Outside in the fields the Heavens open and the shepherds look up astonished to find the music and radiance of Reality all around them. Mary's initiation had been quite different, like a quiet voice speaking in our deepest prayer – 'The Lord is with you!' 'Behold the handmaid of the Lord.' Humble self-abandonment is quite enough to give us God. Think of the tremendous contrast, transcendent and homely, brought together here as a clue to the Incarnation.

The Magi found a poor little family party and were brought to their knees – like the truly wise – before a baby. What a paradox!

The apparently rich Magi coming to the apparently poor child, offering the spirit of adoration.

The shepherds got there long before the Magi and even so, the animals were already in position when the shepherds arrived. He came to His own: the God of nature makes that natural life the material of revelation. His hallowing touch is for the ox and the ass, as afterwards for the sparrows and the flowers. There never was a less highbrow religion or one more deeply in touch with natural life than Christianity, although infinite in its scope. 'Whosoever shall humble oneself, like this little child, shall be greatest in the Kingdom of Heaven' (Matthew 18.4). Without Christ, life is a tissue of fugitive, untrustworthy pleasures, conflicts, ambitions, desires, frustrations and intolerable pain. To accept Christianity as God's supreme self-revelation means accepting the gospel story as touching our lives significantly at every point, because it is conveying God.

*'In the beginning was the Word: and the Word was God . . . the Word became flesh and dwelt among us.' That seems immense, and then we come down to the actual setting of this supreme event – a baby born in the most unfortunate circumstances. The extremes of the transcendent and homely are suddenly brought together in this disconcerting revelation of reality. Absolute surrender and helplessness, the half-animal status of babyhood: all this is the chosen vehicle for the unmeasured inpouring of the Divine Life and Love. The incidents that cluster round the mystery of the Incarnation seem designed to show us His stooping down to us, His self-disclosure. His smile kindles the whole universe; His hallowing touch lies upon all life.

The essence of the Magi is that it's no use being too clever about life. Only in so far as we find God in it, do we find any meaning in it. Cosy religious exclusiveness is condemned in this mystery. It's easy for the pious to join the shepherds and feel in place at the Crib, and look out into the darkness saying, 'Look at those extraordinary intellectuals wandering about after a star; they seem to have no religious sense. Look what curious gifts – not at all the sort of people one sees in church.' Yet the child who began by receiving those unexpected pilgrims had a woman of the streets for His most faithful friend, and two thieves for His comrades at the last. We can learn something of the height, depth and breadth of that Divine generosity into which our narrow, fragmentary loves must be absorbed; the free pouring out of a limitless light – the Light of the World – not its careful communication to those we hold worthy to receive it.

In our souls too the Divine Charity must be incarnate; take visible, tangible form. We are not really Christians until this has been done. 'The Eternal Birth must take place in *you*.' Sometimes Christians seem far nearer to those animals than to the child in His simple poverty and self-abandonment.

We see the new life growing in secret – the child in the carpenter's workshop. This quality of quietness, ordinariness, simplicity – how deeply hidden, how gradual and unseen by us. To contemplate the proportions of Christ's life is a terrible rebuke to spiritual impatience and uppish hurry. Christ's short, earthly life is divided into 30 years for growth and two and a half for action. The pause, hush, hiddenness, which intervenes between the Birth and the Ministry, is part of the Divine method.

In the life of prayer, the Spirit fills us as we grow and make room, keeps pace with us; does not suddenly stretch us like a pneumatic tyre, with dangerous results. The life of the Spirit is to unfold gently and steadily within us. It's an organic process, a continuous Divine action; not a sudden miracle or series of jerks. Therefore there should be no struggle or impatience, but rather a great flexibility, a gentle acceptance of what comes to us. Union with God means such an entire self-giving to the Divine Charity, such identification with its interests, that the whole of our human nature is transformed in God, woven up into the organ of His creative activity, His redeeming

Purpose. We are not to grow in wisdom and stature for our own sakes, in order to achieve what is really a self-interested spirituality. The growth points beyond ourselves, so the teaching, healing, life-changing power of the Divine Love may possess us, and work through us. We must lose our own lives, in order to be possessed by that life: that unmeasured Divine generosity that enters the human world in such great humility. The Holy Child sets up a standard, teaching a great simplicity and self-oblivion, a willingness and readiness to respond to life – to grow and change – according to the overruling will and pace of God.

For discussion

- 'There never was a less highbrow religion or one more deeply in touch with natural life than Christianity, although infinite in its scope.' What thoughts does this statement prompt in you?
- How real does it feel that Christ is born in you? Are there changes you might make to nurture that life?
- Can you think of people who seem to radiate the beauty of Christ's life? How do they nurture Christ's presence in their lives?

Prayer

Lord Jesus, You loved me so much that You emptied Yourself of the glory of Eternity to become human, just as I am. God made flesh, I draw near to You. Be born in me, loving Jesus, and be in truth my *Emmanuel*, Amen.

14

The tempted Christ

In the wilderness temptations, we see the birth of Christ's ministry and the start of a journey that leads, not to revolution or to a palace, but to a cross. Once again, the way of God is revealed as narrower and more humble than we might expect; it is a call to the kind of self-oblivious love that can resist what seem to be the most reasonable, not to say beguiling, suggestions of the 'tempter-spirit'.

How often are we tempted to exercise power and self-importance dolled up in the window-dressing of 'ministry'? Evelyn challenges us about the temptations of (possibly devious) shortcuts to success, influence and self-promotion. For rather than seeking to take charge, we are invited to imitate Jesus' inconspicuous service and enter humbly into a simple, common life, amid all our – and others' – cares and sufferings and weaknesses. And Jesus, our High Priest, who was tempted in every way, will draw alongside us as we too are tempted, pouring out the mercy and grace we need (Hebrews 4.15–16, NIV).

> We begin to see the Mystery through which Christ's life is revealed to us . . . confronted in the wilderness with life's crucial choice and rejecting everything less than God, everything that ministers to self-will. And so emerging into the light of truth . . . teaching the path humanity must follow to God.[1]

> He puts victims back on their feet . . . GOD is sheer mercy and grace; not easily angered, He's rich in love . . . As high as heaven is over the earth, so strong is His love to those who fear

Him. And as far as sunrise is from sunset, He has separated us from our sins.

(Psalm 103.6, 8, 11–12, MSG)

Jesus was taken into the wild by the Spirit . . . the first test: 'Since you are God's Son, speak the word that will turn these stones into loaves of bread.' Jesus answered by quoting Deuteronomy: 'It takes more than bread to stay alive. It takes a steady stream of words from God's mouth.' For the second test the Devil took Him to the Holy City. He sat Him on top of the Temple and said, 'Since you are God's Son, jump.' . . . Jesus countered with another citation from Deuteronomy: 'Don't you dare test the Lord your God.' For the third test, the Devil took Him to the peak of a huge mountain. He gestured expansively, pointing out all the earth's kingdoms, how glorious they all were. Then he said, 'They're yours . . . Just go down on your knees and worship me, and they're yours.' Jesus' refusal was curt: 'Beat it, Satan!' He backed his rebuke with a third quotation from Deuteronomy: 'Worship the Lord your God, and only Him. Serve Him with absolute single-heartedness.'

The Test was over. The Devil left. And in his place, angels! Angels came and took care of Jesus' needs.

(Matthew 4.1–11, MSG)

*Jesus, take us with You into the Wilderness – tempted in all things as we are. And when You had fasted, the tempter came to You – the temptation is to use Your spiritual power to escape this fragile, human nature. Our humanity is constantly calling us from God's interest to self-interest: 'These hard, stony circumstances could be changed – Why suffer? Turn the situation to your advantage: command them to be made bread! Consider your needs – take proper care of yourself!'

What's our answer to that? A refusal to spoil Your dependence on God, Your self-oblivious love: to exploit the Power of the Spirit, even for legitimate ends. That sacred power, which shall feed the five thousand and reveal itself in the breaking of bread, must not be used for itself alone. Lord! Have I ever dared to exploit Your spiritual gifts in my own interest, for my apparent needs? Have I used my communion with You to satisfy my own spiritual hunger?

I'm here to wait on God, to listen to His Voice which feeds me – nourishing my soul in ways I don't understand. Teach me never to taint that union by self-interested consideration – trying to get something out of religion. 'He gave them Bread from Heaven to eat.'[2] Give me tranquil courage – content to await Your gift. I live by what comes from You. Your word proceeding forth from *Your* mouth, at *Your* own time, in *Your* way: not by my deliberate, self-occupied use of the power You give.

Sometimes my need and exhaustion seem great and *You* seem silent: conditions seem stony and hard. Those are the moments when I'm given patience, courage and tranquillity: abiding among the stones in the wilderness, learning dependence on You. Help me remember this in those arid moments, when hungry and thirsty, when the stony facts of life hem me in. May I never try to turn the gifts of religion to my own advantage. May I follow You along the path that runs from the wilderness to the Cross. May I never turn from the path of self-giving to seek advantage for myself; or taint my hours of waiting on You by self-preoccupation.

Now we go with You to the next test of lowly, singleness of heart, to that Temple pinnacle where the Jewish visionaries said the Messiah would appear. The tempter-spirit says in Your heart, 'Have confidence in your own great powers! You are the Son of God. Behave as people expect of the Christ! The hidden years of obedience are over. Give the people signs of Messiahship. Cast Yourself from the pinnacle. Exploit the powers You possess. Have faith! God will support You!' How did You respond to that temptation? That suggestion that faith consists in attempting the impossible, taking risks? You shall not tempt the Lord your God, exploit His promises, try to force His hand.

Have I ever been tempted to try the Temple pinnacle, instead of the straight, narrow path? To turn from simple service – try to get nearer Heaven by a risky, self-chosen route? Have I presumed to climb too high on a dizzy pinnacle of thought or prayer, never meant for me, expecting Your angels to see I'm not harmed? Have I dared to assume that because I'm Your friend and servant, it guarantees special protection when I ignore common sense? Have I expected You to rescue me from my own conceit?

Lord! How different this is from *Your* sublime creatureliness, Your acceptance of the common life limitations, Your steady un-demanding trust in God! I'm not to seek to attract others to God by advertising different religious possibilities – exploiting His generous power. I'm not to be high-minded – practising arrogant other-worldliness. The Temple pinnacle is a lonely place. You won't be waiting for me there. Your method, prayer and disclosure of God take the lowliest path. Your tabernacle among us is in the cave and cottage. I must come down like Zacchaeus, down among the cares, sins, labours and sufferings of ordinary people – *there* we find You. Your Spirit isn't given that we escape life's friction and demands, but so we live the common life as You lived it.

Now we go with You to a high mountain-top. We listen while the tempter-spirit brings before Your human mind the greatness of the world – its teeming races, the possible span of Your powerful influence: all within Your grasp if You listen to the spirit of ambi-tion, act from Your own centre, not from God's heart. 'All these will I give you if you will worship me.' Consider what good You could do if You left this meek, hard service, this local ministry so inad-equate to your talents, and acted on a big scale! All the kingdoms of the world spread out. On one side, the offer of unlimited power to use for God's Purposes; on the other side, quiet teaching, without much apparent result, the narrow sphere, little flock, loneliness, poverty, misunderstanding, a narrow path leading to the Cross. *Humanity* and the full use of the powers given to a human, or *God* and utter dependence on God – the method of the superhuman, or the saint.

There are moments when I have to choose between the quiet, arduous, hidden way and the easy power, obvious spiritual or social success, wide but not deep influence, popularity with its dangers – the shortcut. 'Your Kingdom come!' – obviously that's the way to make it come, do all I can to make it a success. The straight, difficult call of God to deep communion and inconspicuous service; so humble and small a sphere; so few prospects; so little apparent scope – *that* can't be the way the Kingdom will come? So tempting to leave prayer, humility, austerity, the hidden life, tiny deeds of service – no time for that if I'm concerned with all the kingdoms of the world. The tempter-spirit says to me, 'Develop your capacities, take your rightful position, get control of the committee, insist on your point of view, make a success of your life, use your influence and, *then*, give the results to God.'

There are times when all that seems less a temptation than a piece of sensible advice. *You* turned from the kingdoms of the world to the Cross, from the claim of power, exercise of authority, to the acceptance of pain, a living, dying sacrifice; and in that act, You saved the world, lifting humanity to God. Nothing in it for You, everything for Him. The decision that led to the Easter Garden was made in the Judean wilderness. Now, in the beauty and joy of Your Ascended Life – Your Abiding Presence – You bring us back and show us the test and the decision in which it began.

For discussion

- Which of Jesus' three temptations most resonates with what you have experienced in the past and the challenges you currently face? Why?

- Have you ever been 'in charge' of some form of 'ministry' and then, in Evelyn's words, 'given' the 'results' to God? How might this excerpt prompt you to work differently in future?
- Are there any secret temptations you struggle with, that you dare not share with others? Perhaps you could share them with God now in prayer.

Prayer

Lord Jesus, You alone know the pressures and the particular suffering I face; only You can see me as I truly am. Help me avoid the temptation to think too much of myself; to take the easy path; to dodge challenges because I'm too cowardly to face them. Lord, I need You, for I'm fragile and small. Strengthen my spirit so I may grow in courage, endurance, confidence and love, and have mercy on me, in Jesus' name, Amen.

15

The rescuing Christ

In this small vignette, we see Christ coming to His friends on the lake in the midst of a storm. Once more Jesus sets aside His desire for communion with God and His own comfort to help those who need Him. You wonder if the disciples have already forgotten the miracles of Jesus and the power of God they've witnessed, for they appear only to see the power of the wind and waves threatening to destroy them! But then Christ comes, and the situation is utterly transformed through His Presence.

The storm scenario is one we all experience in some form or another. Have you ever felt you were straining at the oars, over-whelmed, exhausted, hopeless? Evelyn encourages us to look to God to support and rescue us at such times, though His action rarely comes in expected or sensational ways. We simply can't predict how God will intervene, but He always does, somehow. He comes. In the following extracts, Evelyn invites us to be channels of His costly, rescuing Love.

> We can't forecast the path God's rescue will take. It is never any use saying, 'I am getting desperate! Please answer my prayer by the next post and send an open cheque.' He *will* answer . . . more probably He will transform and use the un-likely looking material already in hand – the loaves and tiny fishes – looking up to Heaven, blessing it and making it do after all.[1]

> At dusk, dawn, and noon I sigh deep sighs – He hears, He rescues. My life is well and whole, secure in the middle of

danger . . . God hears it all . . . Pile your troubles on GOD's shoulders – He'll carry your load . . .
(Psalm 55.16–19, 22, MSG)

Late at night, the boat was far out at sea; Jesus was still by Himself on land. He could see His men struggling with the oars, the wind having come up against them. At about four o'clock in the morning, Jesus came toward them, walking on the sea. He intended to go right by them. But when they saw Him walking on the sea, they thought it was a ghost and screamed, scared to death. Jesus was quick to comfort them: 'Courage! It's me. Don't be afraid.' As soon as He climbed into the boat, the wind died down. They were stunned . . .
(Mark 6.47–52, MSG)

*Sometimes we are, as it were, in the middle of the lake and the storm breaks, usually from a quarter we don't expect. We feel helpless, making no progress, and say – 'I've gone to pieces; I've no help, no support. *This* can't be a spiritual life.' We begin to lose our grip. The boat's very unstable, steep waves threatening, sky darkening – utter discouragement. It was like that when He 'climbed into the boat' and the 'wind died down' (Mark 6.51, MSG). The situation was transformed by His Presence.

One way or another, life brings every awakening Christian soul this experience. God in Christ intervenes between us and the storm threatening to overwhelm us. His power is brought into action just where our action fails; He comes to the rescue.

Sometimes it's on our soul that He lays His tranquillising touch, stilling the storm; sometimes on our emotional hurly-burly, sometimes on events we think must destroy us, or people and causes we love. We feel sometimes as if we're left to ourselves to struggle. Jesus is praying on the mountain, or asleep in the boat; the waves are getting higher, the night very dark. We begin to lose our nerve for life and no one seems to mind. Certainly life is not made soft for Christians; but it *is* safe.

The disciples were thoroughly frightened, exhausted, soaked, but *not* destroyed. At the critical moment, Jesus climbed into the boat, restoring safety, sanity, peace. Christ stands over against history and in its darkest, most dangerous moments. We receive new revelation of His Power.

This meditation sheds a tranquil radiance on our lives; teaches us in the difficulties, conflicts, tight places, to look for and trust God's rescuing, supporting action – so seldom exerted in ways we anticipate, yet always present, intervening. If Christianity seems hard, it's the hardness of a great enterprise where we get great support. As we go on with the Christian life, we learn the Spirit's power over circumstance; seldom sensationally declared, but always present and active – God in His richness and freedom coming into every situation, overruling the ceaseless stream of earthly events and moulding our souls. His Love penetrates, modifies, quickens our lives.

This general action of God's Power is continuous, but usually unseen. It conditions our lives from birth to death. Now and then it emerges on the surface and startles us – a subtle, ceaseless Power and Love working within the web of events. We ought to think of this far more than we do. The direct action of God lies very thick on the New Testament pages, sometimes intervening in crucial events, sometimes in homely things like wine shortage at a wedding. Sometimes in desperate crises like God's chosen servants brought safely through danger – the prison doors opened. 'The power of God unto salvation' (Romans 1.16, KJV) is the essence of the gospel, not the power of God unto comfort. It's a personal energy, a never-ceasing Presence that intervenes, overruling events. I don't know why we think this strange. It's just our dull, unimaginative stuffiness.

He's always accessible to the personal troubles and desires of His workers, overriding rules where necessary. He's interested in every detail, down to the factory cat. When Christ says God's Majesty and Holiness can both rule Heaven and care for the sparrow and will intervene to help and save, we think that's poetry and paradox. We're too narrow and stupid to conceive the energy of the Unmeasurable Holy, entering our world, changing and modifying circumstances.

There are two sides to every vocation: unconditional giving of self to God's call – 'Here am I; send me' (Isaiah 6.8, KJV) – and the gift of power which rewards the gift of self to God. In Christ's life, how humbly He submitted to the Father's Will, totally absorbed in His business, and to the tests, pressure, suffering that came through circumstances. Yet never in His own interest and never apart from His love and pity for humanity, there is always Power to intervene, save, mould, defeat opposition, transforming the humble accidents of life. In all men and women of prayer, deeply united to God, that double state exists. That handing of self over and the mysterious Power that somehow acts through self in consequence – the right word said, the right prayer prayed. But only in proportion to the self-effacement. The Power of course is God's not ours. When we give ourselves to Him without reserve, we become points of insertion for the rescuing spirit of Love. We are woven into the Redeeming Body so we provide more channels for God.

Are we able, through consecration and self-oblivion, to enter a troubled situation with that gift of peace and power? There's always something of this in people whose lives are hidden in Christ – that deeply surrendered union with God and docility to His requirements: that power of transforming circumstance, exerting a pacifying, saving, compassionate action at our own cost – an essential part of Christ's Pattern.

Dwell on Christ snatching a few hours' solitude for that communion with God, then His vision and knowledge of the poor little boat and its crew. He had left them to themselves and they were already in trouble, caught in a sudden storm. Surely it's in His instant response to that need, not in the wonder and joy of His mysterious prayer, that we're shown His full Majesty and Holy Power. How gentle, humble, uncritical, full of zest we need to be, if that Power is to have a free path! A devotional life tainted by spiritual self-love or self-interest will never convey God's saving power. A self-oblivious, rescuing, helping love is the secret of intercession: willingness to turn from our private communion with God and stretch out the hand of rescue, all the generous love of the redeeming spirit to those caught in the storm. The minister of Christ must always be ready to do that, always on guard against merely enjoying God. I love to think Christ had no special consciousness of performing an abnormal action, that He was inevitably drawn across the stormy lake to the little boat by the overmastering impulse of His compassionate love.

We don't always recognise, who or what that steadying, peaceful Presence is that enters the little boat of the soul, tossing on the waves. But somehow the wind does cease, the reassuring Presence comes. Christ enters the boat, overrules the hurly-burly and sends peace.

For discussion

- When was the last time you found God rescuing you from an overwhelming situation?
- Have you recently responded to a call for help? Did you feel exasperated unwillingness, compassionate love or some other reaction?
- How might you safeguard yourself from burnout and compassion fatigue?

Prayer

O Lord, You have loved and saved me. In Your mercy, please keep on rescuing me! Plant my feet on the rock of Your faithfulness and, through storm and stress, uphold me by Your strength, draw me safely me into Your arms and hold me in Your peace. All love flows from You, so warm my heart with Your Divine fire that I may generously love others, in Jesus' name, Amen.

16

The transfigured Christ

For Evelyn, the Transfiguration is one of the most significant incidents in the Gospel accounts. Christ goes up onto the Mountain of Prayer with some of His friends. They have been faithfully following Him on the basis of the little they have heard and seen, but here the veil of Heaven is parted and they glimpse the radiance of Eternity. The disciples are quite overwhelmed and struggle to communicate what they've experienced. Usually the brightness of God's glory is disclosed in a form adapted to our limitations; this glorious revelation of Christ's person – shining with God's mysterious, transcendent wonder and holiness – changes everything.

Evelyn possessed a vivid sense of God's Majesty and Otherness, imagining Heaven as 'absolutely happy and absolutely dark, to protect us from the blaze of God'.[1] But while on earth, we are to be part of the 'dust-laden air' irradiated by and reflecting God's golden light.[2] In these two extracts, Evelyn ponders Jesus' Transfiguration and Jesus as the Light of the world.

> the absolute Light . . . dazzles us; in its wholeness it is more than we can bear. It needs breaking up before our small hearts can deal with it . . . The universal light of the Father, the interior radiance of the Holy Spirit, linked together in this vision of the Son, so far above us and yet so divinely near . . . We must be receptive, humble and quiet.[3]

> Light, space, zest – that's GOD! So, with Him on my side I'm fearless, afraid of no one and nothing . . . I'll contemplate His beauty; I'll study at His feet. That's the only quiet, secure place

in a noisy world . . . I'm singing God-songs . . . making music
to GOD.
(Psalm 27.1, 4–6, MSG)

Jesus: 'I am the world's Light. No one who follows Me stumbles
around in the darkness. I provide plenty of light to live in.'
(John 8.12, MSG)

Jesus took Peter, James, and John and led them up a high
mountain. His appearance changed from the inside out, right
before their eyes. His clothes shimmered, glistening white,
whiter than any bleach could make them. Elijah, along with
Moses, came into view, in deep conversation with Jesus. Peter
interrupted, 'Rabbi, this is a great moment! Let's build three
memorials – one for you, one for Moses, one for Elijah.' He
blurted this out without thinking, stunned as they all were by
what they were seeing. Just then a light-radiant cloud envel-
oped them, and from deep in the cloud, a voice: 'This is My
Son, marked by My love. Listen to Him.'

The next minute the disciples were looking around, rub-
bing their eyes, seeing nothing but Jesus, only Jesus.
(Mark 9.2–8, MSG)

*The Transfiguration is one of the most astonishing and significant
incidents in the Gospels. Christ, a loved Master to those nearest
to Him, takes them up onto the Mountain of Prayer. And there a
revelation of the hidden mystery of His Life and Presence is suddenly made. He is *changed*. We cannot say much about it because
this experience transcends our ordinary apparatus of thought. We
try to express a splendour that doesn't belong to our order – His
face shining as the sun, which we cannot look at; and His clothing
white as light, 'much whiter than any bleach on earth can whiten
them', says the homely Mark. The One we have read about, tried to

obey and follow, Who's given us His intimate, cherishing love, is *transfigured*. We see in Him the Mystery Incarnate: the Presence that reveals to us more than Itself. And in the shining Presence, Moses and Elijah are talking with Him. The veil of separation parts for a moment and we're allowed to glimpse something of the rich mystery of the Divine Life Christ came to share with humanity.

In the same way, the great truths and sacramental acts and experiences of religion change the very look of natural life, disclosing to us the deeps of the spiritual life. It's important to remember that even the most wonderful of the experiences, and most overwhelming of these truths, are only scraps and samples of an unmeasured reality – the Mystery of the Transcendent pressing through. And, on the other hand, our most fugitive glimpses, experiences and lights, minister God's Mystery to us, but we cannot look steadily at them or describe them when they're withdrawn. The Mystery *is* known: experience *is* transfigured. And then it is over. We look round about and see Jesus only and the life of humble service we're to resume in His Name. But now we know something of that life's hidden mystery and meaning. We've seen His sacred humanity transfigured: a glimpse of what God seeks to do in Him, for the souls submitted to the purifying action of His Love.

For those who come down from the Mount of Transfiguration, life has a different colour. It's revealed its hidden wonder and holiness. Some realise this in one way, some in another. God in Christ has something for every grade of soul: there's no part of life He can't transfigure with His mysterious Presence, so it shines for us in the splendour of the Eternal Light and mediates that cleansing Light to our imperfect souls.

*In Christ, the inaccessible Light we cannot look at is tempered to a radiance we can bear: He, in His Majestic Simplicity, is a beacon lighting everyone that comes into the world and every situation in which He is pleased. 'The Lord shall arise upon you and His glory shall be seen upon you' (Isaiah 60.2), at your own human level, on your own human scale. In Your Light, O Christ, we shall see Light. Not in some lofty and ineffable experience, or some transcendent region foreign to us, but here and now in this crowded, confusing world where we are called to live, with all its imperfections, difficulties, disillusionments.

You walk this world and show us how to live in it; to live as You did, among the greedy, aggressive, disloyal and weak; how to meet and overcome imperfection in the power of rescuing Love. By Your Holy Incarnation, Baptism, Fasting and Temptation, illumine us; pour out the Light of Love upon us.

You change the landscape for us, irradiate and dignify each phase and state of our human nature. You show us its classic pattern, its relationship to God. So teach us to enter more and more deeply into those inexhaustible mysteries of Your incarnate Life, from which the Light shines upon the mysteries of our life.

Your prayer gives its worth and beauty to our prayer. Your ministry sanctifies all our small labours, teaching, healing, rescuing, giving life and comfort – steady, selfless spending of Your powers. Your Passion gives worth and meaning to our suffering, if we unite it with Your total self-offering to God. All the world's pain and sacrificial love are seen in their creative splendour in the Light flowing down from Your Cross.

We turn to the secret world of the Spirit and think of Your Divine Creative Light, cast on our souls, shining in their deeps where we are alone with You: in so far as we open them to Your Light and action in our prayer. Teach us to abide in that Light of Eternity, in simplicity, stillness and peace; asking for nothing, seeking to understand nothing, but absorbed in that selfless adoration of Your glory, which is the heart of prayer. Teach us to endure that same pure, tranquil Light in its convicting holiness, shining on our lives; showing us to ourselves in so far as we can bear it: casting its quiet radiance on our disorder, hardness, selfishness – all that we keep in the dark, shaming us by its revelation of our shabby second-rateness, self-occupation, instability, shirking of sacrifice, our lack of generosity and zest; showing us ourselves in a proportion of which we had never thought, over against the great Reality that surrounds us.

Penetrate these murky corners where we hide memories, and tendencies on which we don't care to look, but which we won't dig up and yield freely to You, that You may purify and transmute them. The persistent buried grudge, the half-acknowledged enmity, which still smoulders; the bitterness of that loss we have not turned into sacrifice, the private comfort we cling to, the secret fear of failure which saps our initiative and is really inverted pride; the pessimism which is an insult to Your joy.

Here, Lord, in this place we bring all these to You, and we review them with shame and penitence in Your steadfast Light. And then cast the ray of Your Truth on all that love and goodness You put in our way, which we have passed by and hardly noticed: the friend we never fully valued: the devotion we took for granted: all the sum of small joys and beauties that outweigh the sorrows and ugliness of which we make so much. Show us Your creation as You see it, and know it to be very good: and add to our penitence the gift of thankfulness, and make us children of Your Light.

For discussion

- Try to imagine what might have been going through the disciples' minds and hearts as they experienced Jesus' transfiguration. How do you think they were changed?
- Is the transfiguration an important part of the Gospel story for you, and if so, why?
- What areas of your life are you reluctant to disclose to Christ's refining light? Why do you think that might be?

Prayer

O God, Your light never fades and Your brightness knows no bounds! Bring me into Your light and illuminate the dark places I try to hide from You, from others and even from myself. Grant me self-knowledge and the grace to begin to shine as You shine, so I may reflect Your light to others, in Jesus' name, Amen.

17

The costly Christ

In this meditation, Evelyn reflects upon the encounter between Jesus and the rich young ruler. He's already paid the price of being a good, respectable Christian and Jesus can see he longs for more. Loving the young man, Jesus challenges him to embrace complete self-abandonment. Evelyn is clear that choosing to follow Jesus is not an easy, pleasant affair. Rather, He demands great renunciation of His followers, and whether our baggage is a desire to be comfortable, or appreciated, or popular or looked up to by others, we need to stop long enough to listen seriously to Christ's demands. It's no good being keen to get on in practical ways in our work if we're not willing to be stripped of the extras we cling to. Truly, the only thing that's really needed on the path to union with Christ is to follow Him.

> Every one of God's ceaseless, inconspicuous invitations and suggestions to our souls should be met step by step by our willed and costly efforts to respond and work with Him, oblivious to self-interest . . . collaborate with Christ as part of His Mystical Body, in His redeeming work . . . sharing in the pain and conflict, the darkness and mystery of the Cross.[1]

> GOD, my GOD, I yelled for help and You put me together . . . The nights of crying your eyes out give way to days of laughter . . . You did it: You changed wild lament into whirling dance . . . I'm about to burst with song; I can't keep quiet about You. GOD, my God, I can't thank You enough.
> (Psalm 30.2, 5, 11–12, MSG)

As He went out into the street, a man came running up, greeted Him with great reverence, and asked. 'Good Teacher, what must I do to get eternal life?' Jesus said . . . 'You know the commandments . . .' He said, 'Teacher, I have – from my youth – kept them all!' Jesus looked him hard in the eye – and loved him! He said, 'There's one thing left: Go sell whatever you own and give it to the poor. All your wealth will then be heavenly wealth. And come follow me.' The man's face clouded over . . . he walked off with a heavy heart. He was holding on tight to a lot of things, and not about to let go.
(Mark 10.17–22, MSG).

*The rich young man came to our Lord and said, 'What shall I do to inherit Eternal Life?' In other words, 'How shall I make my life *real*?'

Use your imagination freely. You are in Palestine, among the little group trying to follow Christ and learn from Him. You see Him as He moves quietly about the country, exercising His strange attractive Power, as He exercises it still – even on those who do not want to surrender to Him. The attraction of the Light of the World, of the One who has the words of Eternal Life, which everyone really longs to hear, never forcing His demands but drawing people like a magnet, by the power of pure self-forgetful Love.

And then we see the young man. Virtuous, prosperous, what we should call quite the best type, with good traditions, a good background. And yet, somehow, dissatisfied. He has felt the attraction, recognised One who can give the only final answer to his problem, and comes *running* – with that rush with which we respond to real beauty, real goodness, real light – and kneels to that revelation of all he longs for and needs to know – as we kneel now. And he asks Jesus what is the price of full life: life in God and for God.

And our Lord quotes him two prices. He quotes first the price of a respectable piety, being a good Christian, a good Churchman. The young man has paid that, but somehow it has not brought what he wanted. And then, looking at him with love, and so desiring for him the full joy of his supernatural inheritance, Jesus quotes him the price of friendship with God – an unreserved consecration, total self-abandonment. Keep the commandments. Follow Me!

Spirit of Jesus! Enlighten my eyes as I dwell with You in the silence, that I may see this choice, the choice which is *You*. And turn my seeing into loving. Where is that scene staged? In my soul. When? Every time I am given a real chance of sacrifice.

'If you would be perfect,' says Christ, 'complete: enter My order, stand by Me, leave all possessiveness, all clutch – personal, intellectual, spiritual clutch – all self-interest, self-love, all the things you think you simply must have. Let comfort, popularity, status, appreciation, even affection, come and go as they will; and so achieve My liberty, My timeless joy.'

In spite of appearances to the contrary, one thing only is needful: the same lesson Martha heard with such astonishment. Only a deep and very humble love can recognise *that* truth.

Jesus, my Master, grant me the recognition which is love. Show me what the attachments and cravings are, which hold me down below your level of total self-surrender, real love. Show me the things that lumber up my heart, so that it cannot be filled with Your Life and Power. What are they? People? Ambitions? Interests? Comforts? Anxieties? Self-chosen aims? *You* know! Show them to me.

I come and kneel at Your feet, and look at the wounds on Your feet and say again, what shall I do? Give me some of Your courage that I may accept the answer, whatever it may be or whatever it costs. For I know that there *is* an answer. I long to be complete in Your service, transmit Your Love, live in Your order.

Take from me all that hinders and teach me to accept in its place all that You accept: the ceaseless demands, needs, conflicts, pressures, misunderstandings – even of those who loved You best.

Help me to discern the particular price You ask and help me to pay the particular price – whatever it may be. Perhaps You have taken away from me the joy of communion with You that once I had: perhaps You ask me to walk for a time without Your felt Presence, in poverty of spirit.

You sent the 70 disciples away from You to do Your Will. They went without question and they returned with joy. So may it be with me. Perhaps You have given me the holy privilege or opportunity of serving Your poor, as Your representative on earth.

Cleanse my service of all selfishness, spiritual or material, all criticism or impatience, all secret desire for consolation, recognition or reward, as I kneel at Your feet. Help me to remember that understanding service is Your standard. The first shall be last and the last shall be first with You.

Let me be content to follow You in anxiety, failure, weariness, darkness, loneliness and contempt. Let me be content to follow You up to Calvary. It is the only path: the way to Eternal Life. But I cannot climb that hill unless I leave my luggage behind. The straight way goes through Gethsemane. Have I enough courage for that?

You did not save the world by Your wonderful teachings or even by Your works of mercy. You saved it by utter self-giving, courage and love: the Cross. Turn my seeing into loving.

Perhaps You have given me a tiny share in Your teaching, hearing, saving or rescuing work, some place on Your staff. May I love those You have given me, to the end, for You and in Your way. May I give and go on giving. May I bear and go on bearing. May I be Your friend, Your servant, Your fellow worker: one of the myriad channels through which Your Divine Charity flows out without hindrance to the world.

Take all that I have and all that I am and subdue it to Your service. For this alone is Eternal Life.

For discussion

Consider these questions prayerfully and answer as honestly as you can. Looking back over the past year:

- In what ways did God test your courage and trust?
- What events tested your supposed good qualities and showed up your weakness under strain?
- What annoyances helped build up your self-control?
- All these 'touches of God' were chances to grow a little more in the Christian life. Did you take them or waste them?

Prayer

Lord, draw me near and tenderly reveal the depths of Your love. Breathe into my soul Your holy desires and make me free, courageous and ready for adventure! I long to live as Jesus lived, doing things as He would have done. Refresh me with Your Presence and Your Power and make me a channel of Your strength and joy to all I serve, in Jesus' name, Amen.

18

The servant Christ

If there's one place Christ may be found, it's where we encounter self-giving, humble service. At their last meal together, Christ prefaces His final teaching by reverently kneeling before these inconstant friends of His and washing the disciples' feet. His action underlines that loving service is not an optional extra but at the very heart of the Kingdom of God – and the way of the Cross. Serving, not being served, is what we must embrace; all those we know or meet are children of God and we are to kneel in spirit before everyone.

Christ washes the disciples' feet . . . patient, gentle, divine action, if we will yield to it, cleanses us . . . Sometimes it is a hard rub, sometimes soft, repeated touches . . . We, in our restlessness, vary between wanting to draw our feet away and wanting to snatch the towel and finish the job ourselves. But it is the discipline of staying quiet and letting God work that we are asked to bear.[1]

Put me together, one heart and mind; then, undivided, I'll worship in joyful fear . . . You, O God, are both tender and kind, not easily angered, immense in love . . . give Your servant the strength to go on . . . gently and powerfully put me back on my feet. (Psalm 86.11–12, 15–17, MSG)

Having loved His dear companions, He continued to love them right to the end . . . and began to wash the feet of the disciples, drying them with His apron. When He got to Simon Peter, Peter said, 'Master, *You* wash *my* feet?' Jesus answered,

'You don't understand now what I'm doing, but it will be clear enough to you later.' Peter persisted, 'You're not going to wash my feet – ever!' Jesus said, 'If I don't wash you, you can't be part of what I'm doing . . . My concern, you understand, is holiness, not hygiene' . . . Then He said, 'Do you understand what I have done to you? . . . if I, the Master and Teacher, washed your feet, you must now wash each other's feet. I've laid down a pattern for you. What I've done, you do.'
(John 13.1–15, MSG)

*The New Testament is full of hints about places and experiences where Christ may be found. There's one place above all where we can never miss Him, and that's where there's a demand on humble, self-oblivious service. He's always showing us, first one way, then another, what it *really* means, in this world, to work for the coming of the Kingdom and offer ourselves as a tool for carrying out God's Will. That means humble, self-oblivious service – self-giving to the point of sacrifice. So we go with Jesus to that Upper Room, where, on the Eve of the Passion, He began to show His disciples what it meant to live the life that tallied with His prayer – *that* Perfect Love – kneeling with great reverence before the sinful, blemished, inconstant, imperfect: treating us as a host treats a guest he honours – washing our dusty feet, as one that serves.

Full of awe and shame we say, 'Lord Christ! Come to me and cleanse me! Cleanse my feet which have followed the dusty paths of my own desires. Cleanse my lips that have often uttered unloving words. Cleanse my hands that have grasped at pleasure and my own advantage, so that I may help the coming of the Kingdom and do the Father's Will. And oh! Cleanse my vision! That I may see within the mysteries of Your Church and the events of my life the ceaseless purifying action of Your generous, patient Love. Help me recognise Your touch, purifying me; Your voice, calling me; Your hand, feeding me, that I may find and recognise You as You come to me in the homely disguise of my daily life, with its ups and downs, opportunities and trials. For it's there You come to me, accepting my limitations, which are not limitations to You.'

Laying aside all sovereignty, You take a towel and gird Yourself. As one that serves, again and again You cleanse the feet marked with mud of the wilderness. You take bread, bless it and break it, and give us the food of angels – Your very Self – to serve the hunger and emptiness of our souls. In all this, everything is for *us*, nothing but humble self-giving for You. Behold the Lord, from where all that Love proceeds!

Teach me to be a transmitter of Your Love. Here, in these humble acts and homely veils of the Divine Generosity, we see and receive the Love of God, transfiguring all things, however earthly, with a supernatural glow.

'I am among you as one who serves' (Luke 22.27, NIV). I exact nothing. I give everything. What can we give but penitent gratitude and love?

Your Church still lives by Your Supernatural Presence, which You showed visibly from Easter to Ascension. Now as then, Your coming is in simple acts of homely service. The Beauty and Power of Your Holy Presence come quite gently within the facts of daily life, to feed, bless, give comfort and peace – the sudden encounter when we think we've lost You; the unexpected Guest who enters, seeking a place; the grilled fish and honeycomb on the shore. And the Presence is still the same.

Come, help me find it in my daily life! Without You I can't exist, and without Your visitation I cannot live. Come! Enter! Cleanse! Feed! Give Peace!

Where did we see You, Lord? Where *You* were most needed – with the healing of the demon-possessed, on the mountain, with the frightened fishermen in the storm, with the sorrowful, remorseful disciples who'd left You to die alone. The Son of Man came not to be ministered to, but to minister; at His own great cost, teaching by service the splendour and omnipotence of Love.

You've said, I've given you an example that you also should do as I've done; that where I am, there my servant should be. For this, not for my personal comfort or spiritual profit, You cleansed me and fed me: cleanse and feed me again and again, that I may be a channel of Your ministry. All things serve You. Grant that I may enter that order!

And who am I to serve? *Your* coming to me in all Your creatures: *Your* Purposes, *Your* Kingdom, *Your* interests, not mine, not even the interests of my soul. *Your* coming, *Your* Birth, *Your* Life, *Your* Dying, is all part of one offering to serve the Eternal Will of God.

In the hour when You approached Your agony, when You needed above all assurance of communion, You gave Yourself in a double movement of generosity to those who were not strong enough to follow where You trod. The humble act of the washing of the feet; the total self-giving of Your Body and Blood. Coming down to the level of our physical life, because we can't rise to the level of Your spiritual life. How deep because simple, and simple because deep, the way You serve souls. Enter my life and use that too.

Teach and help me to enter the life of service which alone is freedom, which accepts humiliation, hardness, poverty, hiddenness, sacrifice, spendthrift love, with a glad generosity, asking nothing, giving itself at last on the Cross for the life and health of humanity. Self-offering in *Your* way, for *Your* purposes; then I am sure to find You. You give me every chance, not one alone, of entering the communion of Your Love.

I can find You in prayer, on the mountain-top, or among the poor, the sinful, the distracted, the workers, the children – wherever there's an opportunity of loving service. There Your saints always found You: here You find, through them, new paths for the coming of Your Love.

So, because I desire to be a servant of the Kingdom, to give my life that God's Will may be done, take me and use me. Teach me to kneel in spirit before all whom it's my privilege to serve, because they're

Your children: to look for the family likeness, however homely and unspiritual the appearance of those to whom I'm sent; however lowly my sphere of service and their needs may be.

I'll be grateful for everything You give me to do, and will lose myself and my will to find You and Your Will in that work, whatever it may be. Willing as you will – to use simple things as instruments of love – the towel and basin, the cup, plate and loaf, willing to do the most menial duties for the sake of love.

For discussion

- In what sphere of life do you most regularly serve others?
- What do you find hard about this and how might God be nudging you to change your attitude to service?
- How do you feel when you respond to seemingly Divine prompts to serve?

Prayer

Lord, You give us a clear example of what we're called to do in washing Your disciples' feet. Help me to recognise the ways in which You come to me and call on me, and grant me the grace to serve You and others with a humble heart. See with my eyes, hear with my ears, think with my mind, love with my heart, and work with my hands through all the happenings of my life, in Jesus' name, Amen.

19

The suffering Christ

Perhaps the deepest mystery of all is that of the suffering God. Christ, incarnated in a real, human body, experiences physical, emotional, psychological and spiritual torment, as He wrestles with the agony of the path ahead. But it is through His willingness to become the 'Suffering Servant' that complete victory is won. Thus the symbol of Christian faith is not the water bowl and towel but the Cross, and it is this we need before us, in both our hearts and our hands. The Cross is our pattern.

> When we see a human spirit . . . choose the path of sacrifice instead of the path of ambition . . . human courage and generosity blazing out on the heroic levels in the shadow of death; the human agony and utter self-surrender of Gethsemane, the accepted desolation of the Cross . . . we recognise a love and holiness which point beyond the world. There we discern that mysterious identity of Revealer and Revealed . . .[1]

> I run to You, GOD; I run for dear life . . . You're my cave to hide in . . . I'm leaping and singing in the circle of Your love; You saw my pain . . . but gave me room to breathe . . . Desperate, I throw myself on You . . . Hour by hour I place my days in Your hand . . . Warm me, Your servant, with a smile . . .
> (Psalm 31.1, 3, 7–9, 14–16, MSG)

Then Jesus made it clear to His disciples that it was now necessary for Him to go to Jerusalem, submit to an ordeal of suffering at the hands of the religious leaders, be killed, and then on the third day be raised up alive. Peter took Him in hand, protesting, 'Impossible, Master! That can never be!' But Jesus didn't swerve. 'Peter, get out of My way. Satan, get lost. You have no idea how God works.' Then Jesus went to work on His disciples. 'Anyone who intends to come with Me has to let Me lead. You're not in the driver's seat; *I* am. Don't run from suffering; embrace it. Follow Me and I'll show you how. Self-help is no help at all. Self-sacrifice is the way, My way, to finding yourself, your true self. What kind of deal is it to get everything you want but lose yourself? What could you ever trade your soul for? Don't be in such a hurry to go into business for yourself. Before you know it the Son of Man will arrive with all the splendour of His Father, accompanied by an army of angels. You'll get everything you have coming to you, a personal gift.' (Matthew 16.21–27, MSG)

*The life of Christ happened to a real man of flesh and bone, accessible to all physical pain. Having roused the hostility of official religion by His generous freedom of love, He was condemned by political cowardice and ecclesiastical malice to a barbarous, degrading death, making that death the supreme triumph of self-abandoned Love.

Human beings are saved by a Love that enters and shares their actual struggle, darkness and bewilderment. God's deep Purposes are worked out through humanity's natural life with its humiliations, conflict and sufferings – its capacity for heroic self-giving, disinterested love – not through ideas and lofty spiritual experiences. Generosity – accepting the vocation of sacrifice, girding itself with lowliness as one that serves, suffering long, never flinching, never seeking its own – discloses its sacred powers to us within our everyday existence.

The Word made flesh, dwelling among us, accepted our conditions, didn't impose His. He took the journey we have to take, with the burden we have to carry. We can't take refuge in our unfortunate heredity, temperament or health, when faced by the demands of the spiritual life. It's as complete human beings, taught and led by a complete Humanity, that we respond to God. A living sacrifice to God's Purposes is the pattern of the Christian's inner life – always something equivalent to the Passion and the Cross.

Suffering has its place within the Divine Purpose, transfigured by God's touch. There's a hard, costly element in all genuine religion – a suffering and love twined so closely together that we can't wrench them apart. If we try to, the love is maimed in the process – losing its creative power – and the suffering remains without its aureole of willing sacrifice. By the Crucifix and what it means to them, Christians must test their position. What we really think about the Cross means, ultimately, what we really think about life. 'Everywhere you will find the Cross,' says Thomas à Kempis. When you've found it, what are you going to do about it? That's the supreme question deciding our spiritual destiny. Are we merely to look at it with horror, or accept it with adoring gratitude, as the soul's unique chance of union with God's Love? The Suffering Servant, bearing its grief and carrying its sorrows, is the One who most perfectly conveys the Divine Charity.

'If anyone would come after me, let them take up their Cross' (Matthew 16.24). The spiritually natural life is very charming and the exclusively spiritual life very attractive. But both stop short of that unconditioned self-giving, that willing entrance into the world's sufferings and confusion, which God asks of rescuing souls. In the Passion, says St John of the Cross, Christ 'accomplished that supreme work which His whole life, its miracles and works of power, had not accomplished – the union and reconciliation of human nature with the life of God'. The first movement of His soul was self-donation to the Father's Purposes: 'I must be about My Father's business' (Luke 2.49, KJV). The last movement of His soul was the utter self-giving, self-oblivious love of the Cross: 'Father, into Your hands I commit My Spirit' (Luke 23.46, NKJV).

'Can you drink of My cup and be baptised with My baptism?' (Mark 10.38). Not unless you care far more about God and His Purposes than you do about your own soul – that's the essence of a spiritual life. Profound submission to God's Will means sooner or later Gethsemane and the Cross. Only those willing to accept suffering up to the limit are capable of giving love up to the limit – the only kind of love which can be used for the purposes of the redeeming life.

Dizzy, safety-first Christianity is useless here. We must accept the world's worst if we're to give it of our best. The wounds given by those we love best, the revelation that someone we trusted couldn't be trusted any more, the peculiar loneliness and darkness inseparable from some phases of the spiritual life – all can be united to the Cross. He invites us to hallow it by the willing consecration of our humiliations, sacrifices and pains; transmuting them into part of that creative sacrifice, that movement of faith, hope and charity, in which the human spirit is most deeply united to God's Spirit. Unless we can do this, our world is chaos – for we can't escape suffering. We never understand suffering till we have embraced it, turned it into sacrifice and given ourselves in it to God. Then, looking from this vantage point upon the Crucifix, we see beyond the torment, darkness and pain. 'O Lord and Lover of Humanity!' – the whole meaning of the Passion is gathered up in that.

Consider Gethsemane, the first prayer of natural agony: 'If it's possible, don't let this happen! I can't face it.' And the second prayer: 'If I must go through with this, Your Will be done.' Because of that scene, at the heart of human suffering we're never alone. We often feel that we make a mess of our suffering – lose the essence of sacrifice, waste our opportunity, fail God, because we can't stand up to it. Gethsemane is the answer of the Divine Compassion to that fear. Christ seems to move with a strange serenity through the scenes of betrayal and trial. If we think of all these events as they actually happened, crowded together, beating one after another in swift succession on a soul unique in its sensitiveness to evil, sorrow and love, we reach a new conviction of the mysterious energy of pain – its necessary presence in all deep religion.

We too, setting our face towards Jerusalem, must serve with humble self-oblivion to the end, meeting every demand on our patience and pity, faithfully dispensing the Water of Life which may pour through us, while leaving our own thirst unquenched. Prayer in darkness and forsakenness, disappearance of everything that could minister to spiritual self-love, humiliating falls and bitter deprivations, the apparent failure even of faith, buffetings of Satan renewed when least expected: they're all part of that long process, which sometimes seems like a plodding journey and sometimes like a swaying battle, through which God's mighty Purposes are fulfilled in human souls.

Comfort and safety-first must give place to courage and love if we're to become travelling agents of the Divine Love. If the road on which we find ourselves is narrow, with bad surfaces and many sudden gradients, it's probably the right route. The obvious, convenient bypass that skirts the worst hill also bypasses the city set upon the hill: the City of the Contemplation of the Love of God.

For discussion

- What does the Cross mean to you?
- How do you view your personal pain and suffering in the light of the Cross?
- What can we learn from Jesus' example of entering into and accepting suffering, yet also standing up for those who suffer unjustly?

Prayer

Lord, on the darkest night ever, You gave Your all to a world that gave its worst to You. Please grant me the courage to follow Your example. You know I am fearful of suffering and inclined to avoid it if I can, so show me how You want me to participate in the coming of Your Kingdom. Help me accept the cost and give me confidence that You'll be there to carry me and comfort me. Jesus, I come to You with expectant faith and pray in Your loving name, Amen.

20

The abiding Christ

In this extract, Evelyn reflects upon the story of the two companions who encounter the Risen Christ on the road to Emmaus. At first they're astonished that this apparent stranger isn't up to date with current news. Jesus takes care not to press Himself upon them; nevertheless, they beg Him to come in and share their meal. As they listen to the One who has the words of Eternal Life and watch Him break bread, their eyes are opened to their guest's identity. Though slow of heart at first, they begin to catch up with the world as seen in God's light. Let's pray we may glimpse such a vision as we invite Christ to abide with us.

> . . . God, and our total self-giving to God – God who is greater than our heart. Once we have truly learned that lesson all else falls into place.[1]

> You've kept track of my every toss and turn through the sleepless nights. Each tear entered in Your ledger, each ache written in Your book . . . God, You did everything You promised, and I'm thanking You with all my heart . . . Now I stroll at leisure with God in the sunlit fields of life.
> (Psalm 56.8, 12–13, MSG)

> 'Abide in Me, and I in you . . . abide in My love.'
> (John 15.4, 9, NKJV)

> Two of them were walking to the village Emmaus . . . deep in conversation . . . Jesus . . . walked along with them. But they

were not able to recognise who He was . . . Then He said to them . . . 'So slow-hearted! Why can't you simply believe all that the prophets said? Don't you see that these things had to happen, that the Messiah had to suffer and only then enter into His glory?' Then He started at the beginning, with the Books of Moses, and went on through all the Prophets, pointing out everything in the Scriptures that referred to Him . . . here is what happened: He sat down at the table with them. Taking the bread, He blessed and broke and gave it to them. At that moment, open-eyed, wide-eyed, they recognised Him. And then He disappeared. Back and forth they talked. 'Didn't we feel on fire as He conversed with us on the road?'
(Luke 24.13–15, 25–32, MSG)

Emmanuel! – God with us! 'I am with You', says the Lord. Help me to remember that, uphill and down dale, in fog and rain and storm. 'Jesus . . . walked along with them. But they were not able to recognise who He was' (Luke 24.16, MSG). Lord! Has it ever been like this with me? Have I been so busied with my own complexity that I missed You in Your simplicity? So fixed on my preconceived ideas about You that I didn't recognise You where You *are*? Have talk and arguments absorbed my attention and drowned Your voice? Have I gone on worrying about religious problems and difficulties while You, transcending all problems and difficulties, quietly kept pace with me on the road?

And presently Christ enters the conversation and says, 'What is it that you are trying to "talk out" and "get straight", to think through?' (Luke 24.17).

And we, still absorbed in our difficulties and notions, say, 'What? Where on earth have You been, that You don't recognise the appalling state of the world – the failure of religion and the problems that confront us – and how hopeless it all looks just now for religious people like us who thought God would intervene and save His people. Things are specially difficult and puzzling for Christians at this moment, and we're having a conference about it, getting more and more confused as we go on.'

Lord! We are often daunted and puzzled, lost in the clash of events, hopes, doubts, disappointments and explanations – too full of prejudice, confused by our own ideas, looking for something large and showy: and so we lose the chance of all You have to give to those who live by prayer and walk with You. Come and walk by us. Our eyes are bound – unable to recognise You. We don't have the clue to history. *You* have the clue.

And then You speak – 'O slow of heart' – not slow of *head*; slow of heart, unloving – 'not to see that it had to be like this if love is All!' And You explain to us the mysterious scroll of human destiny, with all its pain, violence and darkness, never more mysterious than it is just now; its beauty and nobility, cruelty and injustice – expounding it in the light of God. It all looks different then. And our minds are quietened and humbled and our hearts burn with a strange ardour and longing we don't understand. We see that life has meaning only in so far as God is in it: and even its most difficult bits have meaning.

Bitter suffering, treachery, cruelty, mockery, despair; the clash with Roman tyranny and ecclesiastical malice – out of all that anguish and conflict, *Your* saving, radiant spirit of Love and sacrifice must come. Your prophets always knew it. But we are so slow to give up our preconceived ideas; our conventional notions, our feeling that everything ought to go smoothly. Come! Teach us Your mysterious holiness.

The appearance of things often looks very dreadful and hopeless. Injustice and cruelty seem to triumph over goodness. But, in and through them, *You* are walking still, interpreting the Scriptures and the things that concern You, in ways we didn't expect.

Teach us to stop arguing and listen to Your voice: to be simple and quiet, to accept even when we don't understand, or when Your deep and gentle teaching comes into conflict with our deepest prejudice, our longing for comfort, our hard and fast beliefs. Come to us with Your living touch on events; Your sacred hand opening the Scriptures. 'You have the words of Eternal Life' (John 6.68, NIV).

But that's not enough, is it, for Your full revelation? And our full surrender, certitude, delight. That way we may receive Your teaching, but we can't recognise Your Presence, and it's Your Presence that we need. Not when You stand by us as an explanation of life, but when You enter our life with all its homely limitations, as Friend and Guest.

Come in to abide with us, accepting what we have to offer; when the mysterious pilgrim passing through the world who always seems to be going further than we are, towards a strange, unknown destination – turns a chance meeting into something far deeper and closer, something we can never describe and never forget. But that won't happen unless I ask You for it, unless I open the door. Only my desire, constraining You, will make You come in, abide with me, share my small premises, my humble life. The choice is left to me.

Lord! Give me courage and love to open the door and constrain You to enter, offer all my resources, whatever the disguise You come in, even before I fully recognise my guest. Come in! Enter my small life! Lay Your sacred hands on all the common things and small interests of that life, and bless and change them. Transfigure my small resources, make them sacred. And in them give me Your very Self. When out of the heart of my own homely circumstances You feed me – then my eyes are open to the Presence I long for and can never understand.

Lord! Teach me to be more alert, humble, expectant than I have been in the past: ever ready to encounter You in quiet, homely ways. In every appeal to my compassion, every act of unselfish love which shows up and humbles my imperfect love, may I recognise You: still walking through the world. Give me that grace of simplicity which alone can receive Your Mystery.

Come and abide with me! Meet me, walk with me! Enlighten my mind! And then, come in! Enter my humble life with its poverty and its limitations as You entered the stable of Bethlehem, the workshop of Nazareth, the cottage of Emmaus. Bless and consecrate the material of that small and ordinary life. Feed and possess my soul.

For discussion

- In what ways do you think you may be 'slow of heart'?
- When did you last feel the Presence of Jesus in the midst of everyday life?
- Can you think of a time when you failed to recognise Christ and only realised this later?

Prayer

Lord, show me where I'm slow of heart and help me become alert, humble and expectant instead! Open my eyes so I can see You; open my heart so I can love You; unblock my ears so I can discern Your voice, whether in some wonderful religious experience or act of service or (more likely) in ordinary, homely, humble events, for there I'll surely find You. Abide in me, Lord, that I may abide in You, in Your name, Amen.

21

The glorified Christ

Here Evelyn reflects on the encounters between the risen, glorified Christ and His troubled followers as Jesus re-enters their lives. His return and self-revelation make Invisible Love visible once more, and the disciples' fear and doubt are transformed into the Church's archetypal confession: My Lord and my God!

Jesus responds to the disciples' confession by declaring His intention to return to 'My Father and your Father, to My God and your God'. What challenging words these are. For if we dare to take what's implied by them literally, and shoulder our responsibility, they will completely transfigure our lives.

> 'Yours is the Glory' . . . all we can see, love and delight in, all that crushes and bewilders, shames or reassures us, is nothing beside that which we . . . cannot comprehend: 'the mystery which from all ages has been hid in God.' . . . 'Through faith', says St Paul, 'we stand already in grace. But we look towards glory.'[1]

> We fall to our knees – we call out, 'Glory!' . . . GOD makes His people strong. GOD gives His people peace.
> (Psalm 29.9, 11, MSG)

> Jesus said, 'Do not hold on to Me, for I have not yet ascended to the Father. Go instead to My brothers and tell them, "I am ascending to My Father and your Father, to My God and your God."'
> (John 20.17, NIV)

> [Jesus] was taken up and disappeared in a cloud . . . Suddenly two men appeared – in white robes! They said, 'You Galileans! – why do you just stand here looking up at an empty sky? This very Jesus who was taken up from among you to heaven will come as certainly – and mysteriously – as He left.'
> (Acts 1.9–11, MSG)

*The glory of the Divine Humanity seeks out His nervous followers behind the locked doors of the Upper Room, joins them early morning by the lakeside, walks with them on the country road and suddenly discloses Himself in the breaking of bread. It is the One who fed the multitude, pacified the distracted, washed the dusty feet of His followers and who, after giving Himself to be their food, now re-enters their troubled lives; for their sake, not for His own. He comes back to them in a pure impetus of charity, making visible the Invisible Love. 'My Lord!' says St Thomas, seeing, touching and measuring the Holiness so meekly shown to him in his own crude terms; and then uttering the word every awakened soul longs to utter – 'My God!' The cost is that crucifying struggle with natural self-love, that passive endurance of the Divine action, which brings the soul out of the narrow, intense, individual life – even though it's apparently a religious life – into the wide, self-spending universal life of the Divine Charity.

'My Father and your Father' means then, that we are the children of the Eternal Perfect, whose essential nature is generous Love. The Christian is required to be a worker for the Kingdom, a transmitter of the Divine Charity – the great spendthrift action of God. From the first, the transmitters have been ordinary, faulty people like ourselves. 'He gave Himself' to unstable Peter, dubious Thomas, pushful James and John, and Paul, who had persecuted Him. They must have seemed an unlikely collection. But they were surrendered, and so they could be used; woven into the tissue of that Church which transmits the triumphant, all-sacrificing Love.

Christians exist to be the wide-open channels of the inpouring Spirit of Charity, but block Its passage by their interior hardness, spiritual selfishness, apathy and love of comfort and their petty, sterile, religious outlook. They're too timid to risk losing their own lives; to give themselves with undemanding generosity, in order to find the all-generous Life of God – religious pussycats who bask in the golden light. That which we're shown in contemplation, we're required to express in action – by the exercise of Rescuing Love.

*When Christ said, 'My Father and your Father, My God and your God,' He did not say it in the easy way in which we repeat what we think is a consoling text. *Is* it consoling? Is it not tremendous, searching? Doesn't it ask for a tremendous response? We know what His own response was like and what it entailed. Wasn't He making a declaration that must transfigure the whole lives of those who realise all that's implied in it? Sweeping them into a closer union with His vision and joy and sufferings? Conferring on them the tremendous privilege of partnership? Fellow workers with God because co-heirs with Christ. Do let us take that literally!

We each have our place and job in His economy – perhaps in a humble, supple, self-giving life which keeps open in prayer the channel of Love. Christ's Spirit, if I let It, can act through mine – praying in me and above me, as St Patrick said – one more transmitter of God's Power and Love.

And thus we're led up to Christ glorified, revealed at last as the very meaning of the Universe, and down to His ceaseless self-giving in those gifts and graces of the life of prayer and communion, in which His very Life is constantly offered to us. Offered, not merely for our own consolation or improvement, but as the life of the Body, binding us and Him together in the bonds of love to form together that true, invisible Church of which no one knows the boundaries but God alone, which is the eternal living instrument of the Father's Will – a reasonable, holy living sacrifice.

*Glory is the final word of religion, as joy is its final state. The sparks and trickles of the Supernatural which come to us, the hints received through beauty and through sacrifice, the mysterious visitations and pressures of grace reaching us through the conflicts, rebellions and torments of the natural world – all these are earnests of a Wholeness and Perfection yet unseen: as the small range of sound and colour revealed by the senses witnesses to the unseen colour and unheard music of a Reality that lies beyond their narrow span. Behind every closed door which seems to shut experience from us He is standing; and within every experience which reaches us, however disconcerting, His unchanging Presence is concealed. Not in the wind, not in the earthquake, not in the overwhelming splendour and fury of the elemental fire: in none of these, but in the 'voice of gentle stillness' (1 Kings 19.12), speaking from within the agony and bewilderment of life, we recognise the Presence of the Holy and the completing answer to the soul's completed prayer. We accept Your Majesty, we rejoice in Your Power and Glory; but in Your unchanging quiet is our trust. We look beyond the spiritual to Spirit, beyond the soul's country to the personal Origin and Father of its life.

'This is our Lord's will', says Julian of Norwich, 'that our prayer and our trust be both similarly large,'[2] conscious of our own littleness and the surrounding mystery, we reach out in confidence to the All – an upward, outward glance of awestruck worship which is yet entinctured with an utter, childlike trust. *Abba*, Father. Yours are the Kingdom, the Power and the Glory. You are the Beginning and the End of the soul's life.

For discussion

- What do you understand by Evelyn saying that 'glory' is the final word of religion? What does God's 'glory' mean to you?
- How have you contributed – through your heart, soul, mind, strength, secret prayer or outer service – to playing a part in the Body of Christ?

- How are you currently using your God-given energies to contribute to God's Purposes?

Prayer

Eternal God, Your might surpasses our understanding and Your glory cannot be measured. I surrender myself to You completely, and pray You will show me how and where I may best serve You. Risen Christ, think of me, look on me, bless me, enfold me, guide me – and to You be all the glory, in Your name, Amen.

Part 4

HOLY LIVING: EMBRACING GOD'S COMING (GOD HAS COME!)

In Part 4, we shift from gazing at the life of Christ to embracing Jesus' coming to earth, and His continual coming to us every day. Evelyn invites us to respond in worship as we adore God, partake of the Eucharist, seek to be humble, loving and forgiving and share the peace of Christ with others. The Epilogue that closes our meditations expresses our longing for Christ's second coming in glory.

22

Adoration

For Evelyn, the starting point of the spiritual life is adoration. She reminds us that when we encounter God in His majesty and loveliness, adoring worship is our natural response – it is the practice that keeps the unseen, supernatural environment solid and vibrantly real in our lives. Other types of intercession are valuable, but adoration is the antidote to self-obsession. Co-operation through service should come second to worship, so we need to guard against the tendency in churches to focus on committees and meetings rather than on nourishing adoration of God. For the hidden deeps that give us Eternity enable us to give ourselves to Eternity in return.[1]

Adoration is the core practice of the first commandment (love God), and the prerequisite for being able to practise the second (love others). If adoration doesn't colour our prayer, we will miss the essential upward, humble gaze necessary to truly encounter God's Majesty. It is that focus which enables us, small creatures as we are, to transmit God's Love to others.[2]

> What really seems to you to matter most? The perfection of His mighty symphony, or your own remarkably clever performance of that difficult passage for the tenth violin? ... if the music unexpectedly requires your entire silence, which takes priority ... the mystery and beauty of God's orchestration? ... Adoration, widening our horizons . . . redeems the spiritual life . . . gives it a wonderful richness.[3]

GOD is higher than anything and anyone, outshining

everything you can see in the skies. Who can compare with
GOD, our God, so majestically enthroned?
(Psalm 113.4–5, MSG)

Worship GOD in adoring embrace, Celebrate in trembling
awe. Kiss Messiah!
(Psalm 2.11–12, MSG)

*Consider what the word 'adoration' implies: the upward, outward
look of humble, joyful admiration; awestruck delight in God's
Splendour, Beauty, Action and Being, in and for Himself alone,
as the very colour of life. It's an attitude of the soul that purifies
us from egotism straight away. 'Hallowed be Your Name:' not described, or analysed, be Your Name. Before that Name, let the most
soaring intellects cover their eyes with their wings, and adore. God
calls each creature into an ever-deepening communion with Him.
He rides upon the floods. It's because of our own limitations that we
seem only to receive Him in the trickles. Thus an attitude of humble,
grateful acceptance, self-opening, expectantly waiting, comes next
to adoration as the second essential point in our spiritual life. The
spiritually hungry are always filled, if not always with the kind of
food they expected; the spiritually rich are sent away empty.

That's the moral of the story of the publican and Pharisee. The
publican's desperate sense of need and imperfection made instant
contact with God. He had the thing in proportion – 'God, be merciful, be generous, to me, a sinner!' But the Pharisee's accurate
statement of his own excellent situation made no contact with
the Spirit. He was dressed in his own spiritual self-esteem, which
acted like a mackintosh. The dew of grace couldn't get through. 'I
thank You, Lord, that I'm a good Churchman, a good neighbour.'
Along those lines there's absolutely no communion between spirit
and Spirit. Francisco de Osuna says that God plays a game with
the soul called 'the loser wins', a game in which the one who holds

the poorest cards does best. The Pharisee's consciousness that he had such an excellent hand really prevented him from taking a single trick.

*In a real person of prayer, their supernatural environment is more real and solid to them than their natural environment. They are children of God – in the deeps of their soul attached to God, entirely guided by the Creative Spirit in prayer and work. Every Christian starts with a chance of it, but only a few develop it. Called upon to practise in their fullness the two great commandments, you can only hope to get the second one right if you're completely controlled by the first. And that depends on the quality of your secret, inner life, the quality that makes people *catch* the Love of God from you – that means giving time, patience, effort to cultivating your attention. Do you see the great facts and splendours of religion with the eye of an artist and a lover, or with the eye of a person of business? Is your sense of wonder and mystery keen and deep?

Humanity's first duty is adoration; second duty is awe; and third duty is service. Two of the three things for which our souls were made are matters of attitude, of relation: adoration and awe. Unless those two are right, service won't be right. Without that attention to God, all other religious activities will lose their worth. Only a spirituality that puts the whole emphasis on God, perpetually turning to Him, loving itself in Him, refusing to allow even the most pressing work, practical problems, even sin and failure, to distract from God, is a safe foundation for spiritual work. This alone is able to keep alive the awed, adoring sense of the mysteries among which we move – keep our windows open towards Eternity. You can only help others make sense of that world of time and events, which so greatly bewilders us, in so far as you're able to bring into it the spirit of Eternity. It's that Love of God – that Peace and Presence of Eternity for which souls are so hungry; and your power of really feeding them depends absolutely on your own secret life with God.

How many adult Christian workers go on steadily expanding towards Eternity – which testifies to our spiritual vitality? It's essential to give time in this love and prayer. They are 'given', but the gift is fully made our own only by a patient, generous effort of the soul – an ever-deepening, more awestruck adoration of God, plus an ever-widening, more generous outflow of loving interest towards humanity. Develop the prayer in which you are quite supple before God; the prayer that refreshes, braces and expands you and is best able to carry you over the inevitable fluctuations of spiritual level and mood.

The mixed life of prayer and service is a life of looking and working. In the recollected hours of prayer and meditation, you do the looking; in the active hours, you do the working. The time you give to private devotion, feeding and expanding your spirit, making you more supple and a living tool, shall establish adherence to God, safeguarding against a lack of depth, spiritual impoverishment and an insidious tendency to attribute undue importance to external details. Depriving organised Christianity of its due supply of supernatural energy inevitably reduces its redemptive effect. The remedy is to make the private religious life of all over-busy persons aim at more introversion; to make prayer a meditative, recollective type, enabling depth.

That awestruck sense of God's transcendent reality – this prayer of adoration – exceeds all other types in educative and purifying power. It alone can consolidate our sense of the supernatural, conquer our persistent self-preoccupation, expand our spirits and feed and quicken our awareness of God's Wonder. Bathing our souls in the Eternal Light, we return with added peace and energy to the natural world, to do spiritual work for and with God for others. Thus prayer 'swings between the unseen and the seen'. The deepening of the soul's unseen attachments must precede and safeguard the outward swing towards the world. Adoration, not intercession or petition, must be the very heart of the life of prayer. Sometimes we're in such a hurry to transmit that we forget our primary duty is to receive. God's self-imparting through us will be in direct proportion to our adoring love and humble receptiveness. Only when our souls are filled to the brim can we presume to offer spiritual gifts to others.

The remedy for desperate spiritual exhaustion is an inner life governed not by petition but by adoring prayer. When we feel symptoms of starvation and stress, it's time to call a halt; to re-establish the fundamental relationship of our souls with the Father. Only when our hearts are at rest in God, in peaceful and self-oblivious adoration, can we hope to show His attractiveness to others.

For discussion

Evelyn outlines some ways that people engage in adoration of God: meditating on Christ's words and actions in the Gospels; partaking of the Eucharist; 'prayer of aspirations' (repeating aloud short phrases of love, e.g. from the Psalms); spiritual reading (ruminating gently on Scripture or writings by the Saints), singing or participating in worship music.

- Which of these are your preferred spiritual practices?
- What other ways have led you into adoration of God?
- What might enable you to adore God more?

Prayer

Lord, to You belong all glory, honour and power. Show me how to adore You! Increase my love and understanding as You reveal to me more of who You are, and may I praise You with my whole heart, for ever and ever, Amen.

23

Eucharist

If adoration is the heart of prayer, then partaking of the Eucharist is the practice at the centre of our devotional life. The 'Food of Eternity', as Evelyn calls it, provides us with essential spiritual support, reminding us of the great life of the Church and checking our tendency towards individualism.[1] We go to Communion to offer ourselves collectively to God, so we're more fit to mediate His love to others; the sacramental food we receive enables us to grow more fully like Christ.[2] In her down-to-earth manner, Evelyn challenges us not to be spiritual gluttons who are happy to receive from God but keener to feast on a diet of devotional meringues and éclairs than to engage in costly generosity.[3] We will counter this by staying alert and sympathetic to the world's needs.[4]

> Some fragments of bread and a chalice of wine are enough to close the gap between two worlds; and give soul and senses a trembling contact with the Eternal Charity . . . that hand still feeds.[5]

> I want to drink God, deep draughts of God. I'm thirsty for God-alive . . . When my soul is in the dumps, I rehearse everything I know of You . . . GOD promises to love me all day, sing songs all through the night! My life is God's prayer.
> (Psalm 42.1–2, 6, 8, MSG)

> Jesus: 'By eating My flesh and drinking My blood you enter into Me and I into you.'
> (John 6.56, MSG)

*We discover in ourselves a certain capacity for Eternity, but our minds are distracted. We need a pattern – the Eucharistic liturgy – the supreme ritual act, the devotional centre of the Church's Godward life. Here, movement and words combine to produce an art form – the vehicle of her self-offering to God. She gives thanks, offers, adores, breaks and distributes the Bread of Life. Thankful remembrance of the one perfect sacrifice in Christ is the heart of the Eucharistic action. The Bread of Angels is made the pilgrims' food – humble bread and wine.

The fully Christian life is a Eucharistic life. It's conformed to the pattern of Jesus, given in wholeness to God, laid on His altar as a sacrifice of love, and consecrated, transformed by His inpouring life, to give life to other souls. It's adoring, declaratory, intercessory, re-demptive. As fellow workers with the redemptive, cherishing love of the Spirit, Christians are required to live. 'You are the Body of Christ,' said St Augustine to his communicants. That is, in you and through you, the method and work of the Incarnation must go forward. You're meant to incarnate in your lives the theme of your adoration; consecrated, broken and made vehicles of the Eternal Charity.

The liturgy recapitulates the essentials in this life of sanctifica-tion – to repent, pray, listen, learn; then to offer upon the altar of God, to intercede, be transformed to God's Purposes, fed and main-tained by God's Life – each separate soul, unable without the 'rich bread of Christ' to actualise the state to which they're called.

The spirit of adventure, courage, vitality and zest are qualities of the good communicant responding to the awe-filled invitation of God with reverence. 'Blessed be the Kingdom of Father, Son and Holy Spirit!' The worshipper looks to this Kingdom and its interests. It calls humanity to join with angels and archangels, adoring God, fed with heavenly food, reconciled and established in the Kingdom of Love, and subdued to God's guiding, fostering care.

The visible acts and symbols of expressed religion – the offering, blessing and sharing of bread and wine – stand in close relation to life's simple necessities: but they point beyond themselves as holy and significant, for they manifest the deep union of the Church with God. Since the Eucharist is the movement of the Church's life, and represents under symbols life's meaning, the individual soul can move with freedom within its majestic rhythms. Its ritual actions provide a frame in which the most secret responses of the spirit to God can find shelter and support.

The Eucharistic action begins. A Power stronger than ourselves has pressed us to that altar. The Church remembers and gives thanks for God's saving action within the world of time, the Incarnation and Passion of Christ. Humanity with its whole being – soul and body – adores God and gives itself to God.

*We are utterly dependent on Jesus' life as branches on the Vine – His hand still feeding us. The Eucharist represents a perpetual pouring out of Jesus' very life to feed and enhance our small, feeble lives. It is the very heart of Christian worship because it's so rich and far-reaching in significance. It eludes thought, eludes emotion, relies on simple contact, humble and childlike receptiveness, sense quenching soul. It mixes together the extremes of mystery and homeliness, takes the food of our natural life and transforms it into a channel of Divine Life. As Christ gives Himself to feed us, so we have to incarnate something of His all-loving, all-sacrificing soul. If we don't, then we've not really received Him. A spiritually selfish Communion is not a communion at all.

*The breaking of bread, without the cup of the Passion, is only half of the Eucharistic secret. We don't understand that secret till we see the Eucharist and the Cross as two aspects of one indivisible act. The communicant is merely a 'spiritual glutton' unless this rich mysterious action involves a complete, sacrificial self-giving for God's saving Purposes – their tiny contribution to that perfect work of Christ's Eternal Act. The supernatural food is given, the little separate life fed and enhanced, that it may be gathered, itself a lively sacrifice, into the great sacrificial movement of the Divine Life. 'Whoever eats My flesh and drinks My blood remains in Me, and I in them' (John 6.56, NIV). But the energy thus received must be met by the soul's self-oblivious courage, steadfast endurance, staying power. Fervour isn't enough. We need the grit that achieves victory by way of the lonely darkness of the Garden – the terrible darkness that fell at midday upon the Cross. Christianity seeks the increasing Incarnation of His Spirit, and for that sake accepts a standard of purity, renunciation and forgiveness alien to the world's interests.

*The Eucharistic life is profoundly social. The great Intercession, placed at the heart of the Eucharist, reminds us that Christianity accepts the full burden and responsibility of humanity. The Christian communicant goes to the altar as a member of the family. Intercession, therefore, embraces the whole world – not only the hopeful causes but also the hopeless; not only the respectable but also the disgraceful. The confusions, sins and cruelties – people we'd prefer to forget.

*Intercession is offering your will and love that God may use them as channels whereby His Spirit of mercy, healing, power or light, may reach them and achieve *His* Purposes in them. God knows the details – we need not. Probably the best kind of intercession is a quite general offering of oneself in union with our Lord. Christ prays in and through us, lifting up all souls and causes, setting them before God's face – it's our privilege to share that 'lifting-up' process. For some, petition about Tommy's exam or Aunt Jane's bronchitis is the only sort that's real. Perhaps the prayer we make here may find its fulfilment the other side of the world. Perhaps the help we were given in a difficult moment came from a praying soul we never knew! It's all a deep mystery, and we should be careful not to lay down hard and fast rules. The variousness with which grace works is one of the most wonderful things about it. It's a living, personal energy, not a machine, and makes a response of love to all our movements of love – even the most babyish. But our power of interceding for those quite unknown to us is very closely connected with our membership of the Church – it's her total prayer in which we take part.

For discussion

- What intrigued or puzzled you as you read through these excerpts on the Eucharist and intercession?
- If you feel your own experience of Communion has become rather routine, how might it become more meaningful and life-giving?
- When you pray, how conscious do you feel that you are contributing to the prayer of the whole Church? How would you pray differently if this seemed urgent and vital?

Prayer

Lord, please give me the food You know I need; I long to be united with You, for nothing else satisfies. And as I receive the bread and wine, may this nourishment help me grow in You so I can be a channel of Your Love and Grace to others. Once more, I offer up my life as a living sacrifice, for Your name's sake, Amen.

A prayer by Evelyn to use after receiving the Eucharist

Lord, I pray for all who are sick in body or mind – anxious or fearful. May Your gracious hand be ever above them, Your everlasting arms below them, and Your Holy Spirit go with them, lead them onwards to Yourself. Be near them to guard them, within them to refresh them, around them to preserve them, before them to guide them, behind them to defend them, above them to bless them, through Jesus Christ our Lord, Amen.

24
Sacrifice

Evelyn argues that sacrifice is an essential quality of the deepest prayer. When we've truly learned to adore, we will find ourselves more able to pray in the spirit of self-offering and self-abandoned love that Christ's life models for us so wonderfully, and which leads to joy.[1]

Evelyn warns of the danger of wanting the *benefits* of the Passion without being willing to accept a *part* of the Passion. As the Body of Christ, we bear His Cross, and the following three excerpts offer encouragement to enter wholly into the sacrificial life to which we're called.

The Body of Christ . . . depends on the love and sacrifice of the cells that compose it . . . the tiniest act of sacrifice, the humblest act of kindness – is like a pebble thrown into the ocean of Divine Love. It radiates. It affects the whole community.'[2]

I love GOD because He listened to me . . . so intently . . . Oh, GOD, here I am, Your servant, Your faithful servant: set me free for your service! I'm ready to offer the thanksgiving sacrifice and pray in the name of GOD.
(Psalm 116.1, 16–17, MSG)

Take your everyday, ordinary life – your sleeping, eating, going-to-work, and walking-around life – and place it before God as an offering. Embracing what God does for you is the best thing you can do for Him.
(Romans 12.1–2, MSG)

*Sacrifice represents with wonderful richness the many-sided reality of our soul's essential relation to God, of that soul's Eucharistic life of prayer. It begins with a drawing near – a simple, humble, devout movement towards God, acknowledging our sin, but quietly and peacefully, in all our faultiness and inadequacy. And next the humble but absolute and costly offering of our whole self, a willing sacrifice, a gift to God for His Purposes in the sacrifice of prayer. We offer our very life to Him.

Ancient art is full of symbols of that mysterious union of our souls with God in Christ, which is sacrifice – a peaceful spirit of acceptance, and self-offering. Instead of an angry resistance to life, a peaceful submission to God's moulding action felt through life. Instead of self-fulfilment, entire self-giving to Him: an acknowledgment that we owe ourselves to God and can draw near Him only in a spirit of sacrifice; and only as we give ourselves can we experience His transforming Power and share His redeeming Life. We're to draw near, confessing our faultiness and inadequacy, and offer ourselves as we are for His Purposes. Sacrifice is not something wrung out of us about which we get in a fuss, but something we offer peacefully, calmly, with delight. And it's not offered to a God afar off, but to One now intimately present in every fibre of our being; One who is asking for the quiet sacrifice, that He may fill us with His Spirit of Creative Love.

*There are only two ultimate religious attitudes for Christians: that which prays for a share in the *benefits* of the Passion and that which asks for the holy privilege of being allowed a *part* in the Passion. The soul can elect to be a beggar or a giver, a delighted accepter of salvation or a heroic cross-bearer with Christ. But only those who ask for a share in Christ, who can't rest unless they have some tiny part in the struggle against evil and in God's work for souls, know the deepest meaning of His Peace. Most of us must grow a great deal before we have even a glimmer of what Christ really means.

Our response to God's call, our choice of Him, isn't made sure until it leaves the realm of ideas and enters the realm of action. The full Christian life uses the whole of us and is a life of disciplined action, courage and initiative on one hand, and homely, practical, gentle mercy on the other. No life that doesn't offer us the opportunity of that twofold service of courage and compassion fully answers the demands of Christ.

*'Follow me' – follow with complete self-forgetfulness, willingness and delight as His children and friends. It's to these people that Christ's gifts are still offered – to those who abandon softness, waywardness, religious moodiness and spiritual self-will, who fully, faithfully and bravely accept all the various means whereby God disciplines and educates our souls.

It's also to those who don't aim at delightful religious emotions but rather at an increase in the hard, fundamental virtues: humility, endurance, suffering and love, who go on steadily with the life of prayer. Even when it's hard and unrewarded, they plod on, keeping their rule and doing their job faithfully, saying: 'The darkness and the light are both alike to You' (Psalm 139.12, NKJV). It's one thing to come to religion for healing, comfort and support, as crowds did and do, and quite another to accept the terms on which we're admitted to the company of His fellow workers: the discipline of Christ. But it's to that second group that Christ is united in the sacraments and especially imparts His Joys and Peace. Thomas à Kempis is brutally direct when he says, 'Jesus now has many lovers of His Heavenly Kingdom, but few bearers of His Cross, many that are desirous of consolation, but few of tribulation. Many follow Jesus unto the breaking of bread, but few unto the drinking of the Cup of His Passion.' Thousands of us are eating what we suppose to be the Bread of Eternal Life at our brothers' and sisters' expense – basking in the sun. The mystics, with their deep experimental sense of God, and of all that's involved in His service, had a hard name for this kind of thing. They called it 'adoring Christ's Head and neglecting His Feet'. The reign of Christ's Love in individual hearts lights the fire of supernatural charity, compassion and self-sacrifice.

I once read the story of a Brownie who lived in a wood.[3] He had a little wheelbarrow and passed his time in a very moral, useful manner, picking up slugs and snails. Yet there was something lacking in his life. The King of the World passed through that wood very early every morning, and made all things beautiful and new; but the Brownie had never seen Him. He longed to, but something prevented it. He had one cherished possession; a lovely little soft green blanket which had once fallen out of the fairy queen's chariot and which he hadn't been able to help keeping for himself. It was very cold in the wood at night, but the blanket kept him so warm and cosy that he never woke up in time to see the King of the World. And one day there came to him a Shepherd, who looked deep into the soul of the Brownie, and said to him, 'Haven't you yet seen the King of the World?' And the Brownie said, 'No. I do so want to, but somehow I can't manage it.' Then the Shepherd replied, 'But I seem to see something in your soul that keeps you from the Vision; something that looks rather like a blanket!' And at that a terrible fight began in the heart of the little Brownie – a battle between wanting to go on being warm and comfortable in his blanket, and the longing to see the King of the World. Perhaps the ultimate choice that lies before us may turn out to be the Brownie's choice between the Heavenly Vision and the Blanket.

For discussion

- What are you holding on to for comfort, like the Brownie with the blanket?
- How might God be calling you to a life of greater sacrifice? What changes might you make in response to His prompting?
- Reflect on these questions: What have I done for Christ? What am I doing for Christ? And what ought I do for Christ?

Prayer

Lord, give me a spirit of sacrifice. I give You my hands to do Your work. I give You my feet to go Your way. I give You my eyes to see as You do. I give You my tongue to speak Your words. I give You my mind that You may think in me. I give You my spirit that You may pray in me. Above all, I give You my heart that You may love through me, in Jesus's name, Amen.

25
Humility

In reflecting on God's Majesty, we recognise our smallness: glimpsing Eternity humbles us![1] And when we're humble, we're content to encounter God amid the crowd and the messiness of the everyday. We accept all God gives, no matter how odd it might look, rather than try to get the various elements of our spiritual lives – prayer, faith, experience, etc. – all tied up and neatly ordered.

As we adopt Christ's Spirit of humility, we will gradually become freer of the insidious spirit of pride to which we're all so susceptible.[2] Evelyn reminds us that in the book of Revelation, the saints and elders nearest to God cast down their crowns in adoring worship, whereas the lesser fry further off keep on wearing theirs.[3] This echoes the farewell message of Angela of Foligno on her deathbed – 'Make yourselves small! Make yourselves small!'[4]

> Our possession of . . . creatureliness: knowing our own size . . . the self-oblivion and quietness with which we fit into God's great scheme instead of having a jolly little scheme of our own . . . In the family circle there is room for the childish, . . . imperfect and the naughty, but the uppish is always out of place.[5]

> I learned God-worship when my pride was shattered. Heart-shattered lives ready for love don't for a moment escape God's notice.
> (Psalm 51.16–17, MSG)

> When the time came, [Jesus] set aside the privileges of Deity and took on the status of a slave, became *human*! Having

become human, He stayed human. It was an incredibly humbling process.
(Philippians 2.6–8, MSG)

*The upward glance must teach us on one hand our real position, real size and state, over against the great Mount of Holiness. Humbleness and thankfulness must be the graces we ask for first. Pride is the most damaging and most ridiculous of our mistakes, for it wraps the soul in a blanket of unreality and destroys our creaturely sense. Self-esteem is like one of the stiff belts advertised as a support, but which really prevent the muscles from doing their proper work. We get along much better when we exchange it for Christ's yoke.

Perhaps there's no lesson Christ repeated more often and more strongly, first from this angle and then from another, than the silliness, the hopelessness of the ambitious, uppish, self-sufficient attitude, whether in practical or spiritual things. Those stern sayings – 'If anyone wants to be first and aims at it, he will be last.' 'If you want true greatness, be a servant.' That ironic story of the man who takes the best seat at the wedding and has to be asked to move, that has many searching applications, even in the life of prayer. The very real first point in real prayer is humbleness, a natural gratitude for the lowest place. The miracle of religion is that God has mercy on our little souls – we little specks on one small planet. The only thing that matters is the wonder of our relation to God: what He is making; what He wants done. If we do not see the Pharisee's prayer as the comic thing it really was and the publican's abasement as evidence of his sense of God, far more than of his own sinfulness, we are not yet clear of that unreal, human-centred religious world which is from beginning to end the creation of human pride.

Consciously or unconsciously, we've got our eye on the best seat: feel our souls and their prospects matter. And Christ's rebuke to that sort of thing: 'Unless you are transformed and become like small children, you cannot even *enter* the Kingdom of Heaven. Your arrogance, self-assured views, sense of your own size, your scheme for your own future, even for your spiritual future, are an absolute obstruction to God.'

An incarnational and sacramental religion must be drenched in humility. Only the very meek can accept its lessons. Humility will always encounter God along humble paths in humble here-and-now ways. If we're too lofty, we fail to meet Him. The Holy Spirit says, as to Zacchaeus, 'Come down, for I would dwell with you today!' (Luke 19.5). There's no use stopping at the top of the theological tree, out of the way of the crowd and dust. A homely welcome is more important than a good view if we have the Spirit of Christ as our guest.

What about pride of intellect? Our arrogant struggles to get all the interwoven lines of our experience and belief and knowledge clear, to fit them into a pattern; a struggle apt to be more persistent, the more intelligent we are. It's hard for those with mental riches to enter the Kingdom of Heaven (Mark 10.23). We feel somehow it's due to us to get all quite clear; but God doesn't ask us to arrange all the threads of prayer, faith, knowledge and experience in perfect order, and make them into an artistic design. All He asks us to do is to weave up all He gives us, however odd it looks, into the fabric of our lives. God and His Will matter – not us and our satisfaction and enlightenment! Our glimpse of Eternity humbles. We see a bit of the Greatness God is, and we shrink in proportion.

Hilton says there are two types of meekness: 'One is had by working of reason, another is felt by the special gift of love.' The first is mere realism, recognition of our true situation, the facts of the case – that over against the Being of God, we are nothing. But the second is the delighted abasement of adoring love, which is glad of its own nothingness and the greatness of the beloved. Perfect meekness comes from gazing at Christ and means an utter forget-ting of ourselves and our claims and works, the death of intellectual uppishness and pretensions to understanding – like St Thomas when he stopped seeking explanations, gazed at the Risen Christ and could only say – 'My Lord and my God!' It's only when we leave off arrogant effort to understand, that we really begin to understand.

The spirit of humility and the spirit of thanksgiving are one thing. For thanksgiving is our humble answer to God's givingness; acknowledgment of His endless generosity as the One Spirit of all, and putting ourselves and everything else in relation to Him. We say in the confession, 'Almighty God, Maker of all things, Judge of all humanity.' That's precisely what makes the whole texture of our universe and wins the texture of our little souls, *making* them all the time. I, a little creature, can neither make myself nor judge myself. My frenzied self-depreciation and comforting moments of satisfaction, and my notion that I ought to aim at a good spiritual seat, are all tainted by self-esteem. Give me that true humility that abandons all self-judgment, all self-actuated striving and, like a little child, places itself as it is, in the hands of God.

The great Hindu tradition of devotional life, Bhakti, is divided into two opposing schools, called the Cat-way and the Monkey-way. Those who follow the Cat-way say a soul should be as utterly abandoned to God as the kitten which the mother cat carries to safety in her mouth: the kitten does nothing about it at all. Those who follow the Monkey-way say the soul should rather be like a baby monkey, which, knowing its helplessness if left alone, in time of need puts forth all its efforts and clings to its mother with all its little might. Christian humility should on the whole model itself on the baby monkey rather than on the kitten: turn to God and cling to God with an entire, energetic trust, which is founded on the knowledge of His love and our own helplessness.

For discussion

- Looking back over the past year, what experiences or encounters humbled you?

- In which areas of life do you feel you are most prone to pride? Are you aware of blind spots?
- What practical things might you do to help you stay humble towards God and others?

Prayer

Lord Jesus, You humbled Yourself in becoming human and entering our world. Help me to show to others the gentleness, compassion and kindness You demonstrated, and give me grace to resist when I'm tempted to behave proudly or arrogantly. I want to be small! And, like a little child, I place myself in Your hands, trusting in Your Mercy and Love, in Jesus' name, Amen.

26

Love

The two great commandments both speak of love, and for Evelyn, they are inseparable because what lies at the heart of the Eucharistic life is an interweaving of adoring and compassionate love. We don't have the option of loving God and failing to love those around us; if we want to be lovers of God, we must give ourselves to the entire world.[1] But Evelyn reminds us that our love is often disordered: we love the wrong things (displaying pride and greed), we love too much (lust and gluttony), or we love too little (sloth and envy). Even when we *believe* our hearts are truly set on God, spiritual pride and spiritual envy lie in wait for us![2] So we need to pray about our blind spots, for self-love can manifest itself in many subtle forms.

It is in loving others that we practise our love for God, doing our best to reflect God's Love and Grace (deficient though we may often feel in understanding and courage). And in loving others, we learn to love ourselves, for we are one community, all bound together. It's often said that love is more easily caught that taught, and Evelyn speaks of our churches needing to be full of the germs of love.[3] She frequently quotes these words from St John of the Cross: 'When the evening of this life comes, you will judged on love.'[4]

> The old mystics always insist that love and humility are sisters. As we learn about love, we seem to get smaller and smaller and the wonder of God to get greater and greater. The more we realise the fact of this love pouring out from the heart of God to draw all things . . . the deeper grows the love which is demanded of us in return.[5]

God's eye is on those who respect Him, the ones who are looking for His love. He's ready to come to their rescue in bad times; in lean times He keeps body and soul together . . . Love us, GOD, with all You've got – that's what we're depending on.
(Psalm 33.18–19, 22, MSG)

Whoever claims to love God yet hates a brother or sister is a liar. For whoever does not love their brother and sister, whom they have seen, cannot love God, whom they have not seen . . . Anyone who loves God must also love their brother and sister.
(1 John 4.20–21, NIV)

If I speak God's Word with power, revealing all His mysteries . . . but I don't love, I'm nothing.
(1 Corinthians 13.2, MSG)

*No really good work of any kind is ever really done unless it's done in love. St Teresa said the object of this life is to love, work and suffer. The suffering must be accepted in peace, and this can't happen unless both are rooted and grounded in love – a Love ceaselessly present with us, moulding us, inviting us to grow up into greater love. The only real cure for sin lies in an ever more vivid realisation of God's Love. This purifies at the root. All other devices merely deal with results. Only those who have love, or strive after love, have any part in God whatever, or any capacity for serving Him.

Pure love gives and never demands. It's courageous, humble, constant, not worn out with labours, not daunted with difficulties, bravely sticking things out when tired, disheartened and worried. If we give ourselves to God's Purposes, we'll develop such depths of devoted, peaceful love as passes beyond the need of being fed by mere feeling – the chocolate creams of the Christian life. Don't make the mistake of thinking, if you sometimes feel cold and dead, that you don't know how to love.

Be one among the sheepdogs employed by the Good Shepherd. A good sheepdog goes on with its job quite steadily, takes no notice of bad weather, rough ground or comfort – seldom coming back to be stroked. Yet its faithfulness to and intimate understanding with its master is one of the loveliest things. Now and then it just looks at the Shepherd. When the time comes for rest, they are generally found together. Let this be the model of our love.

Real love is homely and gentle. Stupidity, weakness and disappointing narrowness are things we must sometimes bear from those we work among, but God bears them from us the whole time! How often Grace and Love reach us, despite our narrow ideas of Him, our cowardice and refusals. Just think of His wonderful, loving kindness, never despising or refusing any vessel in which we try to catch and hand on the Living Water. After that, can we dare to be critical or impatient with the smallness, weakness and absurdity of those to whom we're sent? Love teaches us that it's above all by admiration and generosity of spirit that we shall help and win them. That vivid consciousness that God is present to us in people's souls – the fallen, degraded, irresponsible, indifferent, bigoted, helpless people who wear us out because they simply won't be helped – God is with them as well as with us. His unguessed, moulding influence is working in, on and all around every soul in ways beyond our conceiving, with apparent results that sometimes puzzle us. If we love and desire to give ourselves to Him, we are bound to give ourselves also to the whole world. God cannot lodge in a narrow heart, and our hearts are as great as our love.

*Envy – failure to delight in the well-being of others – is apt to emerge suddenly from its lair when the bun we had set our hearts on falls to another's share. Jealousy is one of the worst toxins produced by self-love. We've got to love our neighbours as ourselves. 'What is a person but their thoughts and their loves?' These reveal our very selves. The envious outlook is one of the most elusive: it

147

twists, wriggles and often assumes what it thinks an impenetrable disguise. The only way to mortify a sin is to develop the opposite quality. The opposite number of Envy? Brotherly and sisterly love, selfless delight in others' well-being.

In the marvellous symphony of Christ's life, no note is more often struck than a wide, delighted recognition of the best in everyone, from John the Baptist's spiritual greatness to the Magdalen's spirit of love. Children, sinners, very ordinary, stupid people – those with riches He'd like to get rid of because He sees they fill up space where He should be – on all that, our Lord pours out His Love and interest. If we dare to ask for communion with Him, we must get very tiny and try to share that point of view; attune our will to His selfless, unfaltering, loving kindness.

Only the merciful, wide-spreading, self-oblivious love we share with Christ – the love that still radiates from the Cross – will keep us quite secure. The critical glance, rigorous demand for perfection and superior attitude don't enter into God's view of us. 'As a Father pities His children' (Psalm 103.13, NKJV) – what hope and insight into the Divine point of view. We don't know what's in humanity, yet we presume to judge, discount others' little successes, italicise their faults. Yet one thing's certain if we take the Christian view-point: we and our neighbours are bound together in God, made significant only by God, utterly dependent on Him, both parts of the organism in which His Spirit dwells, and on which His Creative Love is ever at work. The realisation of this common possession of God, this common abiding of all our souls in Him, rebukes the contemptuous, envious judgment, shifting life's emphasis from self to God.

God enfolds humanity, and God is revealed in humanity. He may reveal Himself to us in moments of insight, in spiritual communion, but He *does* reveal Himself in our fellow humans. St Francis found Him when he embraced the leper. Brotherly and sisterly love is the appointed school in which we are to learn Divine Love. 'For whoever does not love their brother and sister, whom they have seen, cannot love God, whom they have not seen' (1 John 4.20, NIV). 'The way to My Divinity is through My humanity,' and 'My humanity' unites itself in love with the failures, needs and distresses of humanity and comes to us *there.*

Do we recognise with awe the costly demands on our compassion and service, as opportunities for communion with Christ? Can we see and serve Christ in the person we like least – the person who's got what we want, puts us in the shade, has wounded our love and aroused our bitterness, whose misfortunes seem richly deserved? Or, can those things separate us from the Charity of Christ? If so, whatever our best moments may seem, we haven't entered into the heart of the Eucharistic life – for that is a communion with God and all souls in Him. It's the lovely interweaving of two movements, adoring love and compassionate love, and we can't divorce them without tearing to bits the very fabric of the sacrificial life.

'Blessed are the merciful: for they shall obtain mercy' (Matthew 5.7, KJV). We make our tiny gift of love and mercy to God in His children – worthy or unworthy – and He makes us the unimaginable gift of the ultimate mercy, Himself. Brotherly and sisterly love, the wide-spreading, enlarging spirit of kindliness, is God's appointed preparation of our nature for Divine Love.

For discussion

- If our thoughts and our loves reveal who we are, what have you learned about yourself? How can God and His Purposes become more central in your thoughts than thoughts about yourself?
- Who are you envious of, and why? Ask God to help you love this person generously and sacrificially and delight in their well-being.
- How is your love for God expressed through your love of others? When does it feel most difficult to love others?

Prayer

Lord, teach me to love! There are so many times when I haven't loved my family, friends and colleagues as I ought – let alone my enemies – and I need Your help. May my frozen heart be warmed by Your Divine fire. Pour into my soul Your patience, kindness and compassion, and let Your love work in and through me, to Your glory, in Jesus' name, Amen.

27

Forgiveness

In this excerpt, we read Evelyn's words about forgiveness in the Lord's Prayer. As we've just been pondering, we constantly fail to love as we ought, often because we're simply too caught up in our own concerns. But when we fail to love, we damage ourselves as well as those around us. We need to seek the forgiveness of God and of those we've failed – and to forgive those who have failed us.

We all know that forgiving others can be extremely difficult. We may have been at the receiving end of cruel or selfish behaviour, or simply hurtful thoughtlessness, yet we're asked again and again to extend the mercy and forgiveness God is always showing us. Evelyn helpfully encourages us to consider ourselves as citizens of God's Kingdom of Redeeming Love: forgiveness is 'supernatural', so we should pray for, and expect, a renewal of the Spirit's power in us and, indeed, in the whole Church as we seek to forgive.[1] Evelyn reminds us that the phrase regarding forgiveness in the Lord's Prayer asks that we be treated as we treat others, and we should expect to be taken at our word.

> We are judged by love . . . in every crisis and opportunity of life. Everything which asks us for forgiveness judges us; and only if we pass that examination, can we safely ask to be ourselves reinstated in the kingdom of love.[2]

> If You, GOD, kept records on wrongdoings, who would stand a chance? As it turns out, forgiveness is Your habit, and that's why You're worshipped. I pray to GOD – my life a prayer – and wait for what He'll say and do.
> (Psalm 130.3–5, MSG)

And forgive us our debts, As we forgive our debtors . . . For if you forgive others their trespasses, your heavenly Father will also forgive you. But if you do not forgive others their trespasses, neither will your Father forgive your trespasses. (Matthew 6.12, 14–15, NKJV)

*'Forgive us our trespasses.' Our mixed, half-animal nature, the ceaseless tension between the earth's pull and Heaven's demand, is summed up in these four words. We need light, for our eyes are darkened so we can't see the reality of our state; we need cleansing. Our souls are helplessly sick; sin has sapped their energy. Here stands one who constantly falls short and knows it – blinded by prejudice, self-love; capable of hatred, envy, violence, fear; could've done more and didn't, thought we were strong – turned out weak, trespassed in pursuits of our own ends: a child of God, facing the facts, says, 'Forgive!' Here, in the constant exercise of the Divine economy of penitence and pardon, is one of the strongest links which binds the soul to God.

The Divine forgiveness makes a heroic demand upon our courage. Forgiveness isn't the easy passing of a sponge over a slate. It's a stern, painful process; the reordering of the soul's disordered love. The person doesn't merely soil their own garments, but inflicts damage and suffering on others. The person needs forgiveness of humanity, and of God. The person has abused the sacred gift of freedom, whether corporate or individual, which we entreat God to accept and resolve: and this God can do in only one way – by making the utmost demand on our charity and humility, by a universal application of the law of generous love. 'Forgive us our trespasses, as we forgive them that trespass against us.' We ask with confidence because we are the children of Love and have accepted its obligations. Acknowledging our insufficiency, we are forgiven, if we try to look through the eyes of the Divine pity on the failures of our brothers and sisters in love: forgetting our own injuries, however grievous, and remembering only our common tendency to sin.

There's no lesson Christ loves better to drive home than this disconcerting fact of our common human fragility: which, when we've truly grasped it, kills resentment and puts indulgent pity in its place. Let the person, group, nation that's without sin cast the first stone. God's forgiveness means the compassionate recognition of humanity's weakness and instability. This requires of us constant compassionate recognition of our fellow creatures' instability and weakness.

Hardness is the one impossible thing. Harshness to others in those who ask and need God's mercy sets up a conflict at the very heart of personality, shutting the door upon grace. What's true of individuals is true for the community. This principle makes a demand on our generosity, which only a purified, self-oblivious love can meet. For every soul that appeals for God's forgiveness is required to move over to His side – share the compassionate understanding, unmeasured pity, with which He looks on sinful human frailty.

The Christian doctrine of forgiveness is so drastic and difficult, where there's a deep injury to forgive, that only those living in the Spirit, in union with the Cross, can dare to base their claim on it. It means not only asking to be admitted to the Kingdom of Redeeming Love, but also declaring our willingness to behave as citizens of that Kingdom, even under the most difficult conditions. Cruelty, malice, deceit and violence doing their worst; and seen by us through the eyes of a pitiful God. All this is supernatural. This supreme test; this quiet and genial acceptance of life's wounds, all the deliberate injury and causal damage that comes from lack of love; this prayer from the Cross – Forgive us, as we forgive. Not as we hope to be able to forgive, when our sense of God is more vivid and our sense of injury, our emotional uproar, has died down: but *now*.

Show us, Lord, your indulgent Charity, and we'll try to show it in turn: bear with our faultiness because we're trying to love, ignoring small sums owed us, rights' infringements; unlimited forgiveness –

especially where deceit and injustice triumph, where anger is supposedly justified, and generosity is hard. 'Blessed are the merciful', the generous, 'for they shall obtain mercy' (Matthew 5.7, KJV). The soul can ask for only as much as it's willing to try to give. We say here that we're satisfied if God deals as gently with us, at our worst, as we deal with others at their worst – not more. We ask to be treated as we treat them; and we must expect to be taken at our word. Only a very great Christian can dare to say this prayer without qualification. It's the acid test of a life of charity, of true incorporation in the Body of Christ. There's nothing more purifying, more redeeming than the penitent love awakened by the generous forgiveness of another love. It opens a door in the brick wall which self-esteem has built between itself and God.

There are two perennial situations in which the human creature, individually or as a group, has to exercise forgiveness. First, cases where it considers its established rights have been infringed – trespasses. Second, cases where it considers its own just demands on affection, deference, consideration, possessions or status have not been met – debts. Either by attack or neglect, singly or as a body, the creature's self-love, its pride, is injured; and its anger aroused. But those in whom the life of prayer is operative, whose filial relation with Eternal Love is sure, are required to abandon the standpoint of self-interest, whether personal or corporate; quietly and humbly forgive the trespass, freely remit the debt, if they want to know God's living Peace.

St Teresa makes an easy, prompt forgiveness, in all life's ups and downs, the very test of prayer. Again and again in the Gospels we find Christ insisting on the hopeless situation of the exacting, unforgiving soul, who dares to ask from God what it's not willing to give in turn. St Teresa says, 'God is never strict but always generous. However great our debt, He thinks it a small matter if through it He can gain us.'[3] That generosity principle runs through the New Testament. There, forgiveness is not an effort, a stern duty, but the delighted overflow of a compassionate, self-oblivious charity. It's the joy with which, after a long exhausting search, the tiresome sheep is found, the lost coin hunted down; the delight of the father receiving safely the worthless son who disgraced the family name, wasted its money, remembering family affection only when other resources failed. Even here, forgiveness means music and dancing; no hint of disapproval, all memory of foolish ingratitude drowned in love.

For discussion

- When was the last time you showed forgiveness – perhaps to a member of your family, or a friend, or a colleague at work?
- Are you experiencing any difficulty with someone that has not been resolved because you feel justice has not been done? How do we balance justice and forgiving those who hurt us unjustly?
- How do you feel when you know you've been forgiven?

Prayer

Dear Lord, thank You for the generous, abundant forgiveness You show me. I confess I find forgiveness hard, and I pray now for all those who have hurt me and caused me pain, and for those I have, knowingly or not, caused to suffer. Lord, help me to overcome my tendency towards suspicion, indignation, annoyance or whatever else diminishes my love for others. Have mercy on me, for I am weak and fragile and I greatly need Your help, in Jesus' name, Amen.

28

Peace

The Advent Child was heralded as the Prince of Peace, and on the eve of His betrayal and death, Jesus tells His friends: 'Peace I leave with you.' This gift is not the peace of perfect circumstances – a basking in Divine sunshine, or even a warm religious feeling such as we might experience during prayer. Instead, says Evelyn, peace is a willing acceptance of all that comes to us; a deep tranquillity, persisting through both light and darkness, success and suffering, and one of the surest signs of spiritual health.[1] It comes at a great price – that of the Cross and full, sacrificial abandonment to God.

Evelyn made the maintaining of authentic peace a personal goal, writing in her journal: 'Wherever I go I will say Peace and try to bring Peace'.[2] Like all of us, she was acutely aware of how we need this God-given peace – the climate of Eternity – at our centre, to keep our feet during unsteady times.[3]

That deep tranquillity which we mean by peace of soul is the surest of all signs of spiritual health . . . A peacefulness which persists through success and through suffering alike is the real mark of the Christian soul.[4]

God – You're my God! I can't get enough of You! I've worked up such hunger and thirst for God, travelling across dry and weary deserts. So here I am in the place of worship, eyes open, drinking in Your strength and glory . . . I hold on to You for dear life, and You hold me steady as a post.
(Psalm 63.1–2, 3, 8, MSG)

For to us a child is born . . . And He will be called Wonderful
Counsellor, Mighty God, Everlasting Father, Prince of Peace.
(Isaiah 9.6, NIV)

Peace I leave with you; My peace I give you.
(John 14.27, NIV)

*Obedience, self-denial, humbleness and surrender, from these, says
à Kempis, comes great peace. Without peace, love and joy may easily
become mere emotional effervescence. Peace is, above all things, a
state of the will. It's a calm, willed acceptance of all the conditions
that God imposes upon us, and deepens with our deepening realisation of Him. When we completely transfer the centre of interest
from our ideas to His ideas, then we enter the coasts of peace.

This peace, which St Paul says must crown our love and our joy if
they're genuine, is not merely a nice religious feeling that comes in
times of prayer. It doesn't mean basking in the Divine sunshine like
comfortable pussycats. It's a peace that needs and produces a courageous yet humble kind of love. It means such a profound giving
of ourselves to God – an utter neglect of our opinions, preferences
and rights – as keeps the deeps of our souls within His atmosphere
in all the surface rush, ups and downs, demands and disappointments, joys and suffering of daily life. We cease to matter. Only God
and His work matter. He demands an unmeasured love, and His
response is an unmeasured peace – a peace tested in Gethsemane,
in mockery, insult, misunderstanding, apparent failure, extreme
pain, yet so radical it could be given from the Cross to the dying
thief. 'Not as the world gives' (John 14.27, NKJV), but as the Crucified
gives, at His own cost, now from beyond the world. If we are really
growing towards God, we are growing towards that ideal.

And it's only in such a state of peace that our best work is done.
We don't do it in a state of tension and anxiety. We don't hear God's
voice then. We do our best when we're inspired by that loving

longing of the soul to do the last bit we can for God, being wholly swayed by the Spirit that moulds and uses us. But we shall not work in agitation or strain. So too with our mental obligations, problems and difficulties. We are called upon to deal with those problems up to the limit of our understanding, but always in the atmosphere of 'the peace . . . which surpasses all understanding' (Philippians 4.7, NKJV).

Humbleness, a necessary condition of our love and joy, is the very substance of our peace. The more our sense of God's infinite Reality and steady mysterious Action on life deepens, the less important we and our little efforts and failures become, the greater our peace grows. The golden thread of humility links together the love, joy and peace.

An ever-deepening vision of God's Greatness and our immaturity will help us see things in proportion. It will check 'spiritual ambition', that fussy envy of people who are doing better than ourselves: all the copy-cat sort of holiness. If we can see things in proportion, it will make us very willing, even in the things of the Spirit, to have less rather than more, and to take the lower place. And we shall grow, expand and deepen in proportion to the extent to which we achieve this peaceful forgetfulness of ourselves. Such forgetfulness of self means peace too in the necessary ups and downs of our own spiritual course, accepting what comes from God. When we can say, with no sense of unreality, 'If You will that I be in the light, I shall bless You. And if you will that I be in darkness, I shall bless You. Light and darkness, life and death, praise the Lord,' as à Kempis says, it means that, in the deeps of our souls, our wills are peacefully united to the Holy Will and Love that guides this little world, and gave us the model of the Cross. Merging ourselves in that Will, we find our peace.

Perfect clearness in religion often really just means shallowness, for being what we are, we can't expect to get Eternal Life into sharp focus. Often God and His Peace are more present with us in darkness than in light. We ought to be equally ready for both. It's a very poor sort of faith and love that won't face a dark passage until it knows where the switch is.

St Augustine said that we are nothing else but wills: our inner life is always aiming at something. Generally it's a self-interested something that attracts and keeps our attention. The result – since God made us for Himself and is the only adequate object of our will – is that we are restless. Different and really incompatible things are pulling at our will and our attention, and the result is an interior conflict that saps our strength. The Spirit of God is always pressing our souls to fulfil His mysterious Purpose for each one of us, and our peace consists in obedience to that pressure. Misery and discord come from kicking against it.

*Peace is a word that echoes through the New Testament, nearly always coupled with the idea of a disclosure of truth which adjusts us to life: something that annuls self-interest, anxiety and fear, transcending the apparent injustice and cruelty of life and harmonising our fugitive experience with the all-encompassing Will of God. 'Peace I give unto you' (John 14.27, KJV) – I give the deep, enduring, tranquil peace, the inward quiet of acceptance, the mind stayed on God ready for anything because anchored on His Eternal Reality – indifferent to its own risks, comforts or achievements, sunk in the great movement of His Life. We shall see whether our peace is just a feeling or a fact – a true *fruit* which exists and endures, grows and ripens in the sun and wind of experience. For the Peace of God can co-exist with the sharpest pain, the utmost bewilderment, the agony of compassion which feels the whole awful weight of evil and suffering. 'O Lamb of God, that takes away the sins of the world, grant us Your Peace!' That is a tremendous prayer to take on our lips, for it means peace at a great price; the peace of the Cross, of absolute acceptance, utter abandonment to God – a peace inseparable from sacrifice.

For discussion

- What resonated with you in this extract? Are there phrases you would find helpful to meditate on further?
- Can you think of a time of pain or struggle when you've experienced 'peace beyond understanding'?
- What might help you maintain awareness of your need for God-given peace in your daily life?

Prayer

Father, I long to be held in Your deep peace and to know Your peace in my heart. Lord, it's not always easy to feel peaceful in this unstable world, and I often battle with anxiety, grief and fear. Please uphold me in Your strength and help me abide in You. And, knowing Your deep peace, may I bring healing peace to others, in Jesus' name, Amen.

Epilogue – Come, Lord Jesus!

Waiting is hard. God has shown us that He fulfils His promises, and Jesus has promised He's coming back and 'coming soon'. But although we know Christ's on the way, the 'not yet' is heavy – suffering, anxiety and death are very much a part of our lives during global pandemics. But Evelyn constantly reminds us that our seen reality, our everyday world, is only part of all that is. Eternity constantly presses in on us and will do so more and more, as we open ourselves to God.

For Evelyn, 'come' is the key word for our spiritual lives.[1] We long for Christ to come to us – Come, Lord Jesus! – as He came as a child to Mary. We invite Him repeatedly as we, in turn, come to Him, and we prepare for His great Coming when we shall see Him face to face. In this long Advent, are we watching and waiting for that final Coming? Are we expecting Eternity to break in upon our world once more? That hope is set before us: 'after long woe suddenly our eyes shall be opened; and in clearness of light our sight shall be full'.[2]

It's my hope that something of Evelyn's heart and her profound longing for God have resonated with you through this book. May we all be inspired to step more deeply and intentionally into a life of prayer – into a dance increasingly dominated by the captivating and subtle Music of Eternity. Let us listen to Evelyn one last time, reflecting on the final phrases of the Creed . . .

'I look for the life of the world to come,' or more literally, 'I expect the life of the age that is drawing near.' I expect Eternity as the very meaning and goal of all full human life, especially of the Christian art of living. 'Let us press on to perfection

161

because we have *tasted* of the heavenly gift and the powers of the world to come.'[3]

(Hebrews 6.4–5)

GOD rewrote the text of my life when I opened the book of my heart to His eyes . . . Suddenly, GOD, You floodlight my life; I'm blazing with glory, God's glory!

(Psalm 18.24, 28, MSG)

God . . . I'll be the poet who sings Your glory – and live what I sing every day.

(Psalm 61.1, 8, MSG)

'Look, I am coming soon!' . . . The Spirit and the bride say, 'Come!' And let the one who hears say, 'Come!' Let the one who is thirsty come; and let the one who wishes take the free gift of the water of life . . . 'Yes, I am coming soon.' Amen. Come, Lord Jesus.

(Revelation 22.12, 17, 20, NIV)

*The closing phrases of the Creed call us to ascend in heart and mind to the world of the Country of Everlasting Clearness, and find the meaning of existence there. So, since the Christian life of prayer looks through and beyond Time towards Eternity, finds its fulfilment in Eternity, and ever seeks to bring Eternity into Time, the note that we end on must be the note of inexhaustible possibility and hope. Here those who relax their clutch on 'the' world, and give themselves to the real world of charity, redemptive action and co-operation with God, receive an increasing and astonishing enrichment of existence, a deepening sense of significance in every joy, sacrifice, accomplishment and pain; in fact, a genuine share in that creative Life of God which is always coming, always entering, to refresh and enhance our life.

'This is eternal life; to know You, the one true God' (John 17.3), have our eyes opened – Whom to know is to adore. Christ in His great intercession asked only this for those He loved; this real life, poised in God. 'That they may be in us' (John 17.21) – each tiny separate spirit absorbed in the mighty current of the Divine Charity. 'I in them and You in me, that they may be perfected into one' (John 17.23); this is the consummation we look for, that share in the Life of God prepared for humanity. Ears that can hear, hearts at last capable of a pure, unlimited love. Then that sense of coming to the verge of a world of unbounded realities, which haunts our best moments of prayer and communion, will be fulfilled.

'I look for the life of the world to come' and see hints of it everywhere – a revelation that becomes convincing to others only in the degree in which we suffer and take risks for it, give it priority over self-interest and self-will. This is our terrible privilege – humanity's deepest contact with that unmoved Truth in which the created order is immersed, and which is ever seeking fresh channels whereby to enter, cleanse and refresh the world. To become such a channel is the chief aim of the interior life. We shall achieve it only if a trustful adoration and a limitless self-offering govern our prayer, more and more laying open the very depths of our being here and now to the pressure of that Unchanging God, who accomplishes His creative work by means of the creatures He's made. We are to bring forth the 'fruits of the Spirit' here and now, enmeshed as we are in the complex anxieties of our material and emotional life; ever holding tight to the deep tranquillity of that Unchanging God who comes to us in the 'sacrament of the present moment', and meeting and receiving Him there with gratitude, however baffling the outward form may be.

Our whole life is to be poised on a certain glad expectancy of God; taking each moment, incident, choice and opportunity as material placed in our hand by the Creator, whose whole intricate, mysterious process moves towards the triumph of Charity, and who

has given each living spirit a tiny part in this vast work of transformation. It's a real part, even though its precise character and
importance may not be clear to us; we may not see much result from
it during our own short span, or have any clear view of the strange
design from which the hidden Artist is working. The richness and
splendour of the spiritual universe which surrounds and penetrates
our narrow universe of sense is mostly unperceived by us as we are
now. It's true that as spirits, anchored to this world yet belonging to
that world, we already live within that spiritual universe. But, like
newborn kittens, our eyes are not yet opened to our situation; we
can only vaguely recognise the touch upon the fur.

The narrow limits within which even the physical world is
accessible to us might warn us of the folly of drawing negative con-
clusions about the world that's not seen – an abrupt reminder that
we do really live among worlds unrealised. Our limited spectrum
of colour, with its hints of a more delicate loveliness beyond our
span, our narrow scale of sound: these, we know, are mere chunks
cut out of a world of infinite colour and sound – the world that is
drawing near, charged with the unbearable splendour and music
of the Absolute God. And beyond this, as our spiritual sensibility
develops, sparkles and brief intoxications of pure beauty and mes-
sages from the heart of an Unfathomable Life come now and then
to delight us: hints of an aspect of His Being which the careful piety
that dare not look over the hedge of the paddock will never find. All
this, then, should warn us that humility and common sense both
require an attitude of loving ignorance, of trustful acceptance, as
regards that supernatural life, which is always pressing in on us,
always waiting for us.

The Mystery of God remains a mystery. We can't yet conceive, in
its independent splendour and reality, that world which in moments
of communion we feel to be very near. The life that is ruled by its
own deep longing for God, and is really moving in the direction of
God, is always moving towards that Country. It's true that we can't

conceive all it means and all it costs to stand in that world of purity and wonder from which the saints speak to us; those high solitudes where they taste the mountain rapture, the deeply hidden valleys with a vista of white splendour, torrents of living water, quiet upper pastures and tiny holy flowers. But because we believe in One God, the Eternal Perfect, His Love and Faithfulness and Beauty, so we believe in that world prepared for all who love Him; where He shall be All, in all.

For discussion

- Is 'Come, Lord Jesus!' your prayer? If not, how might you develop your longing for Christ?
- The world to come is something to look forward to. Does this fill you with hope? If not, how do you really feel?
- What hints of the world to come have you already noticed?

Prayer

Lord Jesus, thank You for coming as the Christ-child, and please fill me with longing for Your coming again in glory. Let me not be sleeping but watching! Lord, support me every moment of this life I've been granted. Keep my ears tuned in to any mysterious notes I hear, and when my work is done, in Your mercy, grant me peace to be at last with You, forever delighting in the Music of Eternity. I come! Amen.

Appendix: Editing the excerpts

The excerpts I've chosen for this book are mainly from Evelyn's later writings, primarily her retreat talks, given in the 1920s and 1930s. As they were written a century ago, I have adapted the excerpts to make them more accessible for contemporary readers. Details regarding references for the excerpts are outlined below. In some excerpts, I've drawn from only one reference. In others I've drawn upon two or more references for a particular session. I've started each excerpt with an * so it's clear when a new reference is being utilised.

In editing the excerpts, I haven't changed Evelyn's meaning but simply tried to modernise the language to make her century-old work more accessible to contemporary readers, particularly young people. For example, I've changed 'Thee' to 'You'. I've modernised some archaic words, for example, 'thwarts' to 'prevents', 'beseech' to 'ask', 'holden' to 'bound', 'muzzy' to 'dizzy', 'intercourse' to 'union', 'fortitude' to 'courage'. I've also shaped the material to allow maximum content (sometimes several sources on a topic to enrich the perspectives provided) in the reasonably short 1,000-word excerpts. To achieve this, I've deleted some non-essential words in an attempt to reduce word count, for example, 'fillers' such as 'of course', 'now', 'as it were', and replaced 'the' with a comma. I haven't kept my ellipses in the text, as their inclusion was distracting for readers. Where I've deleted a sentence or sentences within an excerpt, I have generally started a new paragraph. I've also introduced contractions, for example, changed 'He is' to 'He's'. Sometimes I've changed word order to make the meaning more accessible. On rare occasions I've corrected errors from Evelyn's writings published posthumously, for example, changing 'quite' to 'quiet'. As Evelyn consistently used capitals for pronouns referring to God, I've retained these and I've also capitalised pronouns for God and Jesus throughout the other parts of this text, including biblical quotes. In the original texts, Evelyn usually quotes from the King James Version. I have chosen to use a variety of translations for the biblical quotes. Where no translation is provided after a biblical quote, it's because Evelyn has recalled the Scripture 'off the top of her head', so it doesn't fit any particular translation. I have chosen *The Message* paraphrase for the Psalms, as I find the fresh language wakes me up in a way that doesn't always happen with more familiar translations. All short quotes provided before excerpts that aren't Scripture are by Evelyn, unless marked. Any quotes by other writers were included by Evelyn in her own publications and retreat talks. In the prayers, I've synthesised some ideas and short phrases from prayers that Evelyn wrote or selected in her two books of private prayers, published as *Evelyn Underhill's Prayer Book*. I've also included a few prayers from Evelyn's book, *Eucharistic Prayers from the Ancient Liturgies*. References for the prayers and a few questions are outlined below.

Notes

Prologue

1 Grace Adolphsen Brame, ed., *The Ways of the Spirit* (New York: Crossroad, 1994), 176.

2 Carol Poston, ed., The *Making of a Mystic: New and Selected Letters of Evelyn Underhill* (Champaign, IL: University of Illinois Press, 2010), 298.

3 Charles Williams, ed., *The Letters of Evelyn Underhill* (London: Longmans, Green and Co., 1943), 252.

4 Evelyn Underhill, *The Golden Sequence* (London: Methuen and Co., 1933), x.

5 Evelyn uses this quote in our first excerpt. It's from Tagore's poem 'Have You Not Heard His Silent Steps?' *Gitanjali* XLV 'Song Offerings'. Tagore was a Bengali poet who won the Nobel Prize for Literature in 1913.

6 Margaret Cropper, *The Life of Evelyn Underhill* (Woodstock, VT: SkyLight Paths Publishing, 2003), 102.

7 Christopher J. R. Armstrong, *Evelyn Underhill (1875–1941): An Introduction to Her Life and Writings* (London: Mowbray, 1975), xii.

8 Williams, ed., *Letters*, 207, 152; Bernard Holland, ed., *Baron Friedrich von Hügel: Selected Letters* (London: J. M. Dent and Sons, 1926), 60.

9 Underhill, *Golden*, x.

10 Evelyn Underhill, *The Spiritual Life* (New York: Harper and Brothers Publishers, 1937), 12.

11 Evelyn Underhill, *The Fruits of the Spirit. Light of Christ. Abba* (London: Longmans, 1960), 70.

12 This poem by John Donne is provided at the beginning of the
   second volume of Evelyn's prayer book (see *Evelyn Underhill's
   Prayer Book*, 54). It was also a verse placed on the porch as a
   keynote for one of Evelyn's retreats (Menzies, 'Memoir' in *Fruits*, 13).

1 God's perpetual coming

1 Evelyn Underhill, *The Golden Sequence* (London: Methuen and Co.,
   1933), 88.
2 Evelyn Underhill, *Concerning the Inner Life* (London: Methuen and
   Co., 1927), 27.
3 Rabindranath Tagore, 'Have You Not Heard His Silent Steps?'
   Gitanjali XLV 'Song Offerings'.
4 Wisdom of Solomon, 18:14–15a, KJV Apocrypha.

2 Mighty symphony of the Triune God

1 Evelyn Underhill, *Concerning the Inner Life* with *The House of the
   Soul* (London: Methuen and Co., 1950), 141.
2 Evelyn Underhill, *The Golden Sequence* (London: Methuen and Co.,
   1933), 82.
3 Evelyn Underhill, *Concerning the Inner Life* (London: Methuen and
   Co., 1927), 13.

3 Eternal Love brooding over creation

1 Evelyn Underhill, *The School of Charity. The Mystery of Sacrifice*
   (London: Longmans, Green and Co., 1950), xv–11.
2 Quoted by Underhill in *School*, 12.

4 Wakening to God's Eternal Action

1 Evelyn Underhill, *The School of Charity. The Mystery of Sacrifice*
   (London: Longmans, Green and Co., 1950), 72.
2 Underhill, *School*, 44–5.
3 Underhill, *Fruits*, in Evelyn Underhill, *The Fruits of the Spirit. Light
   of Christ. Abba* (London: Longmans, 1960), 23.

4 Evelyn Underhill, *The Golden Sequence* (London: Methuen and Co., 1933), 151, 91.

5 Underhill, *Golden*, 150.

5 Father, hallowed be Your Name

1 Evelyn Underhill, *The Golden Sequence* (London: Methuen and Co., 1933), 110.

2 Evelyn Underhill, *Concerning the Inner Life* (London: Methuen and Co., 1927), 46–9.

3 John of the Cross, *The Spiritual Canticle*, 2nd Version, stanza xii (footnote in *Abba*, 17).

4 Jean-Pierre de Caussade, *L'Abandon à la Providence Divine*. Ca. II, I. (footnote in *Abba*, 19 in *Fruits*).

6 Your Kingdom come

1 Evelyn Underhill, *Abba*, in Evelyn Underhill, *The Fruits of the Spirit. Light of Christ. Abba* (London: Longmans, 1960), 6.

2 Evelyn Underhill, *Light of Christ* (London: Longmans, Green and Co., 1944), 92–3.

3 Underhill, *Abba*, 34.

4 Evelyn Underhill, *The Spiritual Life* (New York: Harper and Brothers Publishers, 1960), 75, 77, 79–80.

7 Advent waiting

1 Underhill, *Fruits*, in Evelyn Underhill, *The Fruits of the Spirit. Light of Christ. Abba* (London: Longmans, 1960), 59.

2 Dana Greene, ed., *Fragments from an Inner Life: The Notebooks of Evelyn Underhill* (Harrisburg, PA: Morehouse, 1991), 55.

3 Underhill, *Fruits*, 60.

4 Grace Adolphsen Brame, ed., *The Ways of the Spirit* (New York: Crossroad, 1994), 77.

8 Advent expectancy

1 Evelyn Underhill, *The School of Charity. The Mystery of Sacrifice* (London: Longmans, Green and Co., 1950), 8.

9 Advent hope

1 Evelyn Underhill, *Concerning the Inner Life* with *The House of the Soul* (London: Methuen and Co., 1950), 124, 130.

10 Advent silence

1 Grace Adolphsen Brame, ed., *The Ways of the Spirit* (New York: Crossroad, 1994), 56.

2 Brame, *Ways*, 80–1.

11 Advent prayer

1 Evelyn Underhill, *Light of Christ* (London: Longmans, Green and Co., 1944), 43.

2 Evelyn Underhill, *The Degrees of Prayer* (London: Edward Wilson House, 1960; first printed 1922), 4.

12 Advent contemplation

1 Dana Greene, ed., *Fragments from an Inner Life: The Notebooks of Evelyn Underhill* (Harrisburg, PA: Morehouse, 1991), 58.

2 Evelyn Underhill, *The Golden Sequence* (London: Methuen and Co., 1933), 169.

3 Evelyn Underhill, *The School of Charity. The Mystery of Sacrifice* (London: Longmans, Green and Co., 1950), 54.

4 Evelyn Underhill, *The Life of the Spirit and the Life of Today* (Harrisburg, PA: Morehouse, 1994), 13.

5 Greene, ed., *Fragments*, 100.

6 Evelyn Underhill, *Light of Christ* (London: Longmans, Green and Co., 1944), 27.

Part 3

1 Evelyn Underhill, *Mixed Pasture* (London: Methuen and Co., 1933), 71.

13 The Incarnate Christ

1 Evelyn Underhill, *The School of Charity. The Mystery of Sacrifice* (London: Longmans, Green and Co., 1950), 39, 65.

2 Underhill, *School*, 40–1.

14 The tempted Christ

1 Evelyn Underhill, *Light of Christ* (London: Longmans, Green and Co., 1944), 97–8.

2 John 6.31 (cf. Exodus 16.4; Psalm 78.24).

15 The rescuing Christ

1 Evelyn Underhill, *Light of Christ* (London: Longmans, Green and Co., 1944), 71–2.

16 The transfigured Christ

1 Margaret Cropper, *The Life of Evelyn Underhill* (Woodstock, VT: SkyLight Paths Publishing, 2003), 167.

2 Evelyn Underhill, *The School of Charity. The Mystery of Sacrifice* (London: Longmans, Green and Co., 1950), 45.

3 Evelyn Underhill, *Light of Christ* (London: Longmans, Green and Co., 1944), 29–30.

17 The costly Christ

1 Evelyn Underhill, *The Life of the Spirit and the Life of Today* (Harrisburg, PA: Morehouse, 1994), 189, 191.

18 The servant Christ

1 Grace Adolphsen Brame, ed., *The Ways of the Spirit* (New York: Crossroad, 1994), 209–11.

19 The suffering Christ

1 Evelyn Underhill, *Man and the Supernatural* (London: Methuen and Co., 1927), 122.

20 The abiding Christ

1 Evelyn Underhill, *Light of Christ* (London: Longmans, Green and Co., 1944), 55.

21 The glorified Christ

1 Underhill, *Abba*, in Evelyn Underhill, *The Fruits of the Spirit. Light of Christ. Abba* (London: Longmans, 1960), 84–85; Romans 5.2.

2 *Revelations of Divine Love.* Cap. 42 (*Abba*, 87). I used the word 'similarly' to replace 'alike'.

22 Adoration

1 Lucy Menzies, ed., *Collected Papers of Evelyn Underhill* (London: Longmans, Green and Co., 1946), 103–4.

2 Evelyn Underhill, *The Golden Sequence* (London: Methuen and Co., 1933), 84.

3 Evelyn Underhill, *The Spiritual Life* (New York: Harper and Brothers Publishers, 1960), 64–5.

23 Eucharist

1 Charles Williams, ed., *The Letters of Evelyn Underhill* (London: Longmans, Green and Co., 1943), 260.

2 Grace Adolphsen Brame, ed., *The Ways of the Spirit* (New York: Crossroad, 1994), 166, 96.

3 Evelyn Underhill, *The School of Charity. The Mystery of Sacrifice* (London: Longmans, Green and Co., 1950), 40.

4 Evelyn Underhill, *The Golden Sequence* (London: Methuen and Co., 1933), 189.

5 Underhill, *School*, 67.

24 Sacrifice

1 Evelyn Underhill, *The Golden Sequence* (London: Methuen and Co., 1933), 169, 167.

2 Grace Adolphsen Brame, ed., *The Ways of the Spirit* (New York: Crossroad, 1994), 188.

3 Daisy Sewell, *Visions in Fairyland* (London: H. R. Allenson Limited, 1921).

25 Humility

1 Underhill, *Mount*, 27.

2 Evelyn Underhill, *Light of Christ* (London: Longmans, Green and Co., 1944), 63.

3 Underhill, *Fruits*, in Evelyn Underhill, *The Fruits of the Spirit. Light of Christ. Abba* (London: Longmans, 1960), 36.

4 Underhill, *Fruits*, 36.

5 Underhill, *Fruits*, 35–6.

26 Love

1 Quoted by Underhill in *The School of Charity. The Mystery of Sacrifice* (London: Longmans, Green and Co., 1950), 101 (Élisabeth Leseur).

2 Evelyn Underhill, *The Mount of Purification* (London: Longmans, Green and Co., 1960), 14–15.

3 Lucy Menzies, ed., *Collected Papers of Evelyn Underhill* (London: Longmans, Green and Co., 1946), 102.

4 Quoted by Underhill in *School*, 63.

5 Grace Adolphsen Brame, ed., *The Ways of the Spirit* (New York: Crossroad, 1994), 61.

27 Forgiveness

1 Underhill, *Fruits*, in Evelyn Underhill, *The Fruits of the Spirit. Light of Christ. Abba* (London: Longmans, 1960), 71–2.

2 Underhill, *Abba*, 69.

3 Teresa of Avila, *The Way of Perfection*, Cap. 26. 9 (footnoted by Evelyn in *Abba*, 70).

28 Peace

1 Grace Adolphsen Brame, ed., *The Ways of the Spirit* (New York: Crossroad, 1994), 71.
2 Dana Greene, ed., *Fragments from an Inner Life: The Notebooks of Evelyn Underhill* (Harrisburg, PA: Morehouse, 1991), 92.
3 Underhill, *Fruits*, in Evelyn Underhill, *The Fruits of the Spirit. Light of Christ. Abba* (London: Longmans, 1960), 19.
4 Brame, ed., *Ways*, 71.

Epilogue

1 Evelyn Underhill, *The Golden Sequence* (London: Methuen and Co., 1933), 22.
2 Quoted by Underhill in *The School of Charity. The Mystery of Sacrifice* (London: Longmans, Green and Co., 1950), 101.
3 Underhill, *School*, 101.

References for excerpts and prayers

1 God's perpetual coming

Underhill, *Fruits*, 62–4; Brame, ed., *Ways*, 111, 113–15. Prayers: Underhill, *Fruits*, 52 (St John Chrysostom).

2 Mighty symphony of the Triune God

Underhill, *Spiritual*, 14–15, 17–23, 25–7, 30; Underhill, *Life*, 11; Underhill, *Golden*, 174, 176; Underhill, *School*, 16. Prayers: Wrigley-Carr, ed., *Prayer Book*, 83 (*Veni Creator Spiritus*, final stanza).

3 Eternal Love brooding over creation

Underhill, *Meditations*, 43–52. Prayers: Underhill, *Meditations*, 48; Wrigley-Carr, ed., *Prayer Book*, 48–49 (Margaret Cropper), 80.

4 Wakening to God's Eternal Action

Underhill, *Golden*, 16–18; Underhill, *Spiritual*, 33–5, 42–4, 46, 50–1, 53–6, 58; Underhill, *House*, 99, 102, 103, 108; Underhill, *School*, 17–20. Prayers: Wrigley-Carr, ed., *Prayer Book*, 41 (Fénelon).

5 Father, hallowed be Your Name

Underhill, *Abba*, 18–27. Prayers: Wrigley-Carr, ed., *Prayer Book*, 56 (St Augustine), 65.

6 Your Kingdom come

Underhill, *Abba*, 28–38. Prayers: Wrigley-Carr, ed., *Prayer Book*, 70, 77.

7 Advent waiting

Underhill, *Mount*, 12; Underhill, *Light*, 25–6; Underhill, *Mixed*, 76–7, 80; Underhill, *Spiritual*, 83–123; Underhill, *Spiritual*, 88–9; Prayers: Wrigley-Carr, ed., *Prayer Book*, 80, 13, 92–3, 26.

8 Advent expectancy

Brame, ed., *Ways*, 128–33. Prayers: Brame, ed., *Ways*, 116 (From Roche, *Mysteries of the Mass in Reasoned Prayers*, 92); Wrigley-Carr, *Prayer Book*, 77, 29–30 (P. Charles).

9 Advent hope

Underhill, *House*, 124–37. Prayers: Wrigley-Carr, ed., *Prayer Book*, 108, 114.

10 Advent silence

Underhill, *Ways*, 50–3; Underhill, *Fruits*, 1–2; Underhill, *Light*, 26–34. Prayers: Wrigley-Carr, ed., *Prayer Book*, 40 (Grou), 24.

11 Advent prayer

Underhill, *Degrees*, 8–10; Williams, ed., *Letters*, 73; Underhill, *Concerning*, 56–7, 60–2; Williams, ed., *Letters*, 270–1. Prayers: Wrigley-Carr, ed., *Prayer Book*, 55, 18–19 (E. B. Pusey).

12 Advent contemplation

Underhill, *Concerning*, 19; Underhill, *Life*, 161–2; Williams, ed., *Letters*, 127; Underhill, *Degrees*, 5–6, 10–12, 15. Prayers: Wrigley-Carr, ed., *Prayer Book*, 41 (Fénelon), 22 (Richard Rolle), 34 (St Augustine), 30 (St Anselm).

13 The Incarnate Christ

Underhill, *Light*, 36–40; Underhill, *School*, 39–50. Prayers: Wrigley-Carr, ed., *Prayer Book*, 33, 74 (Luis de Leon); *Eucharistic*, 111 (Mozarabic Missal).

14 The tempted Christ

Underhill, *Meditations*, 31–41. Prayers: Underhill, *Meditations*, 41–2.

15 The rescuing Christ

Underhill, *Light*, 70–8. Prayers: Wrigley-Carr, ed., *Prayer Book*, 52, 67–8, 82.

16 The transfigured Christ

Underhill, *Mount*, 70–1; Underhill, *Meditations*, 59–63. Prayers: Wrigley-Carr, ed., *Prayer Book*, 36–7; Underhill, *Meditations*, 63 (Dawn Office, Eastern and Leonine Churches); Wrigley-Carr, ed., *Prayer Book*, 57, 51 (Newman); Underhill, *Mount*, 71.

17 The costly Christ

Underhill, *Meditations*, 5–11. Questions: Underhill, *Mount*, 8. Prayers: Wrigley-Carr, ed., *Prayer Book*, 68, 70, 22–3.

18 The servant Christ

Underhill, *Meditations*, 23–8. Prayers: Wrigley-Carr, ed., *Prayer Book*, 73–4; Underhill, *Meditation*, 29.

19 The suffering Christ

Underhill, *School*, 51–62. Prayers: Wrigley-Carr, ed., *Prayer Book*, 78, 65.

20 The abiding Christ

Underhill, *Mount*, 94–9. Prayers: Underhill, *Mount*, 12; Wrigley-Carr, ed., *Prayer Book*, 45 (Margaret Cropper).

21 The glorified Christ

Underhill, *School*, 65–72; Underhill, *Light*, 93–5, 98; Underhill, *Abba*, 85–7. Questions: Underhill, *Light*, 95. Prayers: Wrigley-Carr, ed., *Prayer Book*, 84 (Jeanne-Françoise de Chantal), 81.

22 Adoration

Underhill, *Spiritual*, 61–9; Underhill, *Concerning*, 14–47. Prayers: Wrigley-Carr, ed., *Prayer Book*, 29.

23 Eucharist

Underhill, *Mystery*, 'Introduction' (no page numbers), 14–19; Underhill, *Light*, 88–9, 96; Underhill, *House*, 103–4; Underhill, *Mystery*, 33; Williams, ed., *Letters*, 292–3. Prayers: Wrigley-Carr, ed., *Prayer Book*, 41, 25–6 (*Imitation* IV.3), 106–7.

24 Sacrifice

Underhill, *Mount*, 38–41. Brame, ed., *Ways*, 124–7; Underhill, *Mixed Pasture*, 70–94. Questions: Underhill, *Ways*, 98. Prayers: Wrigley-Carr, ed., *Prayer Book*, 43; Underhill, *Ways*, 101 (Lancelot Andrewes).

25 Humility

Underhill, *Mount*, 19–23, 26–8. Question: Underhill, *Mount*, 8. Prayers: Wrigley-Carr, ed., *Prayer Book*, 38; Underhill, *Mount*, 29.

26 Love

Underhill, *Ways*, 60–3; Underhill, *Mount*, 42–7, 48–51. Prayers: Wrigley-Carr, ed., *Prayer Book*, 59, 52 (St Anselm), 44, 28 (Lancelot Andrewes).

27 Forgiveness

Underhill, *Abba*, 60–7. Prayers: Wrigley-Carr, ed., *Prayer Book*, 42–3 (*Imitation* IV.9).

28 Peace

Underhill, *The Ways*, 72–5; Underhill, *Fruits*, 12–13. Prayers: Wrigley-Carr, ed., *Prayer Book*, 55, 45 (St Ethelwold), 49 (*Prière simple*), 49.

Epilogue

Underhill, *School*, 101–11. Prayers: Underhill, *Eucharistic*, 109 (Gelasian Sacramentary); Wrigley-Carr, ed., *Prayer Book*, 86.

References

Armstrong, Christopher, J. R. *Evelyn Underhill (1875–1941): An Introduction to Her Life and Writings.* London: Mowbray, 1975.

Brame, Grace Adolphsen (ed.). *The Ways of the Spirit.* New York: Crossroad, 1994. (*Ways*)

Cropper, Margaret. *The Life of Evelyn Underhill.* Woodstock, VT: SkyLight Paths, 2003.

Greene, Dana (ed.). *Fragments from an Inner Life: The Notebooks of Evelyn Underhill.* Harrisburg, PA: Morehouse, 1991. (*Fragments*)

Menzies, Lucy (ed.). *Collected Papers of Evelyn Underhill.* London: Longmans, Green and Co., 1946. (*Collected*)

Poston, Carol (ed.). *The Making of a Mystic: New and Selected Letters of Evelyn Underhill.* Champaign, IL: University of Illinois Press, 2010. (*Making*)

Underhill, Evelyn. *Concerning the Inner Life.* London: Methuen and Co., 1927. (*Concerning*)

Underhill, Evelyn, *Concerning the Inner Life* with *The House of the Soul.* London: Methuen and Co., 1950. (*House*)

Underhill, Evelyn. *The Degrees of Prayer.* London: Edward Wilson House, 1960. (First printed 1922.) (*Degrees*)

Underhill, Evelyn. *Eucharistic Prayers from the Ancient Liturgies.* Longmans, Green and Co., 1939. (*Eucharistic*)

Underhill, Evelyn. *The Fruits of the Spirit. Light of Christ. Abba.* London: Longmans, 1960. (*Fruits*)

Underhill, Evelyn. *The Golden Sequence.* London: Methuen and Co., 1933. (*Golden*)

Underhill, Evelyn. *The Life of the Spirit and the Life of Today.* Harrisburg, PA: Morehouse, 1994. (*Life*)

References

Underhill, Evelyn. *Light of Christ*. London: Longmans, Green and Co., 1944. (*Light*)

Underhill, Evelyn. *Man and the Supernatural*. London: Methuen and Co., 1927. (*Man*)

Underhill, Evelyn. *Meditations and Prayers*. London: Longmans, Green and Co., 1949. (*Meditations*)

Underhill, Evelyn. *Mixed Pasture*. London: Methuen and Co., 1933. (*Mixed*)

Underhill, Evelyn. *The Mount of Purification*. London: Longmans, Green and Co., 1960. (*Mount*)

Underhill, Evelyn. *The School of Charity. The Mystery of Sacrifice*. London: Longmans, Green and Co., 1954. (*School*) (*Mystery*)

Underhill, Evelyn. *The Spiritual Life*. New York: Harper and Brothers Publishers, 1960. (*Spiritual*)

Williams, Charles, (ed.). *The Letters of Evelyn Underhill*. London: Longmans, Green and Co., 1943. (*Letters*)

Wrigley-Carr, Robyn, (ed.). *Evelyn Underhill's Prayer Book*. London: SPCK, 2018. (*Prayer Book*)

The Big Church Read

Did you know that you can read

Music of Eternity

as a Big Church Read?

Join together with friends, your small group or your whole church, or do it on your own, as Robyn Wrigley-Carr leads you through the book.

Visit **www.thebigchurchread.co.uk** or use the **QR code below to watch exclusive videos from Robyn Wrigley-Carr** as she explores the ideas and themes of *Music of Eternity*.

The Big Church Read will also provide you with a reading plan and discussion questions to help guide you through the book.

It's free to join in and a great way to read through *Music of Eternity*!

CPSIA information can be obtained
at www.ICGtesting.com
Printed in the USA
FSHW022001241121
86454FS